Femi G. Olumofin

A Holistic Method for Assessing Software Product Line Architectures

I0009601

Femi G. Olumofin

A Holistic Method for Assessing Software Product Line Architectures

Rationale, Concepts, Stages, and Case Studies

VDM Verlag Dr. Müller

Copyright © 2007 VDM Verlag Dr. Müller e. K. and licensors
All rights reserved. Saarbrücken 2007
Contact: info@vdm-verlag.de
Cover image: www.purestockx.com
Publisher: VDM Verlag Dr. Müller e. K., Dudweiler Landstr. 125 a, 66123 Saarbrücken, Germany
Produced by: Lightning Source Inc., La Vergne, Tennessee/USA
        Lightning Source UK Ltd., Milton Keynes, UK

Copyright © 2007 VDM Verlag Dr. Müller e. K. und Lizenzgeber
Alle Rechte vorbehalten. Saarbrücken 2007
Kontakt: info@vdm-verlag.de
Coverbild: www.purestockx.com
Verlag: VDM Verlag Dr. Müller e. K., Dudweiler Landstr. 125 a, 66123 Saarbrücken, Deutschland
Herstellung: Lightning Source Inc., La Vergne, Tennessee/USA
        Lightning Source UK Ltd., Milton Keynes, UK

ISBN: 978-3-8364-2290-1

to Dr. David O. Oyedepo

and to my wonderful family: Favour, Grace and Faith

Contents

Foreword   xiii

Preface   xv

1 Introduction   1
   1.1   Motivation   1
   1.2   Software architecture   3
   1.3   Software product lines   4
   1.4   Problems of product line architectures assessment   5
   1.5   Contributions of this book   7

2 Related Work   9
   2.1   Architecture   9
   2.2   Product lines   12
   2.3   SPA assessment   14
        2.3.1   Software Architecture Analysis Method (SAAM)   14
        2.3.2   Architecture Tradeoff Analysis Method (ATAM)   16
        2.3.3   Active Reviews for Intermediate Design (ARID)   17
        2.3.4   Cost Benefit Analysis Method (CBAM)   17
   2.4   PLA assessment   17
        2.4.1   Product Line Software Engineering - Domain-Specific Soft-
              ware Architecture (PuLSE-DSSA)   18
        2.4.2   VTT PLA evaluation framework   19
        2.4.3   Family Evaluation Framework (FEF)   19
        2.4.4   Assessing architecture analysis methods 19

3 HoPLAA: Rationale and main concepts   21
   3.1   Architecture Tradeoff Analysis Method (ATAM)   22
        3.1.1   The steps of ATAM   22
        3.1.2   The ATAM output   25
   3.2   Approaching the problem of PLA assessment   26
   3.3   The HoPLAA concepts   27
        3.3.1   Dual-stage assessment steps 27
        3.3.2   Extension of quality tradeoff analysis 29
        3.3.3   Context-dependent scenario treatment   30
        3.3.4   Qualitative analytical treatments for variation points . . . 30
        3.3.5   Quality conformance checking technique   31

3.4   The Steps of HoPLAA 32
       3.4.1   Stage I: CA Evaluation 33
       3.4.2   Stage II: Individual PA Evaluation 34
3.5   Evaluation 35

4 Case Study I: The AGM product line   37
4.1   Overview 37
4.2   Scope, requirements and qualities 37
4.3   Stage I: CA Evaluation 38
4.4   Stage II: PA Evaluation 42

5 Case Study II: The btLine product line   45
5.1   Overview 45
5.2   Scope, requirements and qualities 45
5.3   Stage I: CA Evaluation 47
5.4   Stage II: PA Evaluation 52

6 Comparing architecture assessment methods   57
6.1   Approach 57
6.2   Initial comparison of HoPLAA and ATAM 58
6.3   Comparison using parameters from Kazman et al., 2005 62
6.4   Discussion of results for the case study I 63
6.5   Discussion of results for the case study II 64

7 Conclusions and future work   67
7.1   Summary of research 67
7.2   Future work 69
7.3   Conclusions 69

List of Abbreviations   71

References   73

Index   79

List of Figures

2.1   Activities and dependencies in a SAAM evaluation.   15
3.1   ATAM inputs, outputs, and participants.   22
3.2   A sample ATAM utility tree.   23
3.3   HoPLAA inputs and outputs.   28
3.4   Pertaining to the stage breakdown of the HoPLAA method.   28
4.1   Enhanced AGM CA deployment diagram.   39
4.2   A view of the Brickles architecture.   43
5.1   Topology of the btNet scheme and product interconnections.   46
5.2   The CA for the btLine family.   48
5.3   The product architecture for the *btMain* product.   52

List of Tables

3.1   Sample ATAM utility tree.   24
3.2   Sample ATAM scenario analysis.   24
3.3   Scenarios list voting table.   25
6.1   Comparison profile for PLA assessment methods.   59
6.2   A comparison of HoPLAA vs. ATAM.   60

Foreword

The development of quality software is a challenging task. One of the recently pursued avenues in this area is the concept of Software Product Line Architectures: architectural frameworks for a family of software products with a common asset base, but aimed at different market segments. In order to fully leverage the promised or expected benefits of Software Product Line Architectures, we need methods and measures to assess their quality, and tools to help us in that assessment. While a number of techniques for the assessment of software architectures have been proposed, few of them are capable of addressing the specific needs of software product line architectures.

This might be attributed to the relative novelty of the product line architecture concept, but also to its inherent complexity and the lack of a widely accepted development methodology. Probably the single greatest obstacle is the dual role of the architecture in a software product line: there is the 'baseline' architecture for the product line as a whole, and there are separate architectures for each of the product instances. As might be expected, there is significant overlap between those roles, but there are important differences as well – and both should be evaluated: baseline architecture for its robustness and generality, instance architectures to make sure they meet the specific behavioral and quality requirements of the product at hand. However, existing architecture assessment methods provide little guidance as to the extent of the overlap or the importance of the differences, and they are unable to single out the differences that need special attention.

This was, in shortest possible terms, the problem that Femi Olumofin addressed in his research, putting to good use his years of practical experience in designing and deploying software systems based on the product line architecture paradigm. His main idea, to adapt an existing architecture assessment method for single architecture products to the task of assessing software product lines, has evolved into a comprehensive and promising assessment framework. This framework provides crucial information about the features of the software product line architecture that are relevant to the designer, and it does so in a succinct, effective, and efficient manner. This short but nevertheless informative and readable book presents the main tenets of the framework, which will enable software architects to design better software product line architectures and, thus, ultimately help improve the process of designing and developing the complex software systems of today.

Vojislav B. Mišić
Winnipeg, Manitoba, Canada

Preface

Product line development is gaining wider acceptance as an alternative approach for improving the quality of software products and the productivity of the development process. Software product lines are produced from a common asset base which may include requirements, design specifications, and source code. Common examples of product lines in other areas include mobile phones, cars, consumer electronic devices such as TVs and the like. All of the items in a product line share the same basic functionality. However, each individual product may have some specific characteristics of its own or these characteristics may be shared among some, but not all, of the products in the line.

The large-scale reuse of software architecture is at the core of the product line approach to software development. The product line architecture (PLA) artifact is first developed and is subsequently subjected to an assessment process using an architecture assessment (or analysis or evaluation) method. The analysis process ensures that key architectural constraints and goals are satisfied before the PLA is used as the basis for further development of the software products. So, successful product line development depends on the availability of established techniques for architecture development as well as architecture assessment; which is our focus in this book.

Interestingly, the problem of PLA assessment has not been given adequate attention as compared to PLA development. This is partly due to the misconception that PLAs are no different from one-at-a-time or single products architectures (SPAs). So, the traditional architecture assessment methods that were developed for SPAs are being used to assess PLAs; which unfortunately cannot yield satisfactory results. This book is written to change how we approach and attempt PLA assessment exercise. It provides a more detailed focus on the peculiarities of the PLA and the areas that needs to be explored to obtain a satisfactory assessment. Based on the findings and our coverage of the characteristics of existing SPA assessment methods, we developed a new method called HoPLAA (Holistic Product Line Architecture Assessment).

The HoPLAA extends the ATAM (a SPA method) into a holistic approach suitable for the assessment of the dual forms of architectures in a PLA (the core architecture or CA and the individual product architectures or PAs). The concepts, rationale and steps of this new method are introduced in this book. Examples are presented in the form of assessment-focused case studies and they demonstrate how the HoPLAA method can be used to assess PLAs in real life situations. This book also covers materials on why specialized assessment method are more beneficial for product line architecture assessment using the particular case of the HoPLAA method.

Organization of this book

The chapters in this book are organized as follows:

Chapter 1 covers introductory materials to this book and provides a brief background on software architecture and software product lines. It will help motivate readers and help them understand the context and importance of the problem addressed by this book – assessment of software architectures in a product line development environment.

Chapter 2 provides a review of previous research that is related to this work. It covers more materials on software architecture and software product line assessment. In addition, it provides a review of some commonly used architecture assessment methods and an indication of the suitability of each approach for product line architecture assessment. A brief introduction to techniques for evaluating an architecture assessment method is also presented.

Chapter 3 explores the rationale and concept of the holistic method presented in this book – HoPLAA. It begins with a description of the ATAM method and the underlining concepts of the HoPLAA method. This was followed by a detailed description of the stages and steps of the HoPLAA method.

Chapters 4 and 5 present two case study results of product line architecture assessments, conducted using the HoPLAA method presented in this book.

Chapter 6 attempts an objective evaluation of the HoPLAA method. It provides detailed comparison of the HoPLAA method with ATAM. The comparison was presented using a profile developed as part of this work, and also using the parameters presented in Chapter 2 for evaluating an architecture assessment method. The advantages of using HoPLAA based on the result of the two case studies were also presented.

Finally, Chapter 7 concludes the book with a summary of the work presented and an outline of possible directions for future research.

Acknowledgements

I would like to express my profound appreciation to a number of individuals that contributed directly or indirectly to the work that resulted into this book.

First, I want to thank Dr. Vojislav B. Mišić for all his supportive roles. Although only my name appears on the cover of this book, the work is a by-product of my collaboration with him. My interest in software architecture and product lines has continued to soar right from the time he introduced me to the field during my master's years at the University of Manitoba. Thanks for supervising and funding my graduate research.

I am indebted to my family who were very supportive all these while; my darling wife, Favour, for your love, understanding and care. You are a woman among many. I love you. And to my little angels, Grace and Faith, thanks for the joy you bring to this whole process of writing.

I want to acknowledge my parents Mr. Folorunso Olumofin and Mrs. Esther Olumofin for the foundation laid in supporting my pursuit of computer science as an undergraduate major. I also appreciate the goodwill and untiring prayers of my mother-in-law Elder Rachael Sani. And to my siblings and sister-in-laws, thanks for being there: your support and companionship are second to none.

I am grateful to the leadership and the brethren at The Redeemed Christian Church of God, Winnipeg for the privilege of fellowship.

Thanks to Dr. David Oyedepo, the President of the World Mission Agency for your obedience, dedication, and exemplary lifestyle. I am one of those multitudes that have been inspired to pursue and live a life of purpose.

Finally, I return all the glory to God for His abundant grace. Thank you Lord Jesus, I owe all to you.

Femi G. Olumofin
Winnipeg, Manitoba, Canada
July 2007

1

Introduction

1.1 Motivation

Quality and productivity are two of the most important motivations of software engineering research in the last three decades. On one hand, today's businesses and the most versatile systems are increasingly dependent on high quality software. The software quality is described in terms of attributes such as modifiability, performance, availability, security, and portability, among others. On the other hand, software developers are hard pressed to find ways to develop high quality software in the shortest time and with the lowest cost. This quest for more productive ways of developing quality software has been the underlaying motivation for software-based research since the birth of software engineering in 1968.

On the quality motives, existing research results and industrial practice evidence has shown the software architecture as the appropriate vehicle for addressing software quality problems [Dijkstra, 1968; Bass, Clements and Kazman, 2002; IEEE, 2000]. The *architecture*, which refers to the high level structural design of a software system, helps shift developer's focus from complex and intricate low-level elements like the data structure and algorithm of the software, to high-level constructs such as components, connectors and topology. A component is the unit of computation; a connector mediates interactions (dependencies or method call in programming terms) between components; topology is the overall structural description or configuration of a software system in terms of components and connectors [Shaw and Garlan, 1996]. This global, high level view of software designs simplifies developers' understanding of the solution. It consequently enables them to exploit architectural abstractions for reasoning about and determining quality attributes of a software system even before the first line of code is written. The architecture can be used in this way to gain insight into the quality attributes that the software system will possess and exhibit when actually deployed.

Research on ways to improve software production productivity has not been deprived of success. In particular, reuse has been identified as one of the most important concepts to implement, regardless of the level of granularity; at the architectural level, reuse can lead to an order-of-magnitude improvement in software development productivity [Bass et al., 2002; Bosch, 2000; Clements and Northrop, 2005; Clements and Northrop, 2002]. Architecture-based reuse occurs at a more conceptual level than the better known code reuse.

Reuse can be undertaken on an ad hoc, one-at-a-time basis by simply identifying the opportunity to reuse some of the design artifacts. However, the real benefits of reuse can only be realized when reuse is undertaken in a systematic, planned, top-down fashion. At the architecture level, planned reuse involves using a common architecture as the basis for developing a family of related software products popularly called *software product lines* or *product families* . The software product line refers to a set of systems developed from a common core asset base [Clements and Northrop, 2002]. Common examples of product families in other areas include mobile phones, cars, consumer electronic apparatus such as TVs and the like. All of the items in a product family share the same basic functionality. However, each individual product may have some specific characteristics of its own. (These characteristics may be shared among some, but not all, of the products in the family.) For instance, an automobile manufacturer can systematically assemble several unique versions of the same car model from a common body and engine block but using different transmissions (automatic or manual) and an optional navigation system. The cars are built from the same core asset (or architecture), but are differentiated by optional and alternative features.

The concept of product lines enables manufacturers to reap the benefits of reusing the common asset base while being able to cater to the specific needs of particular market segments. Thus, it provides the foundation for improving productivity and quality while reducing cost.

The architecture plays a central role in both one-at-a-time and product line development. In both cases, the architecture, once defined, needs to be evaluated for suitability to fulfill its intended purpose, and to maximize the likelihood of actually achieving the quality attributes goals defined for the solution. The process of evaluating the architecture is called architecture assessment (analysis or evaluation) [Clements, Kazman and Klein, 2002; Bass et al., 2002] . In this book, we will use the terms *assessment*, *evaluation*, and *analysis* interchangeably. In more formal terms, architecture assessment validates the design artifacts, i.e., checks whether we are building the right solution, much like code reviews and testing validates the actual program code [Clements and Northrop, 2002].

There are a number of methods that have been developed for the assessment of single product architectures (SPAs). This includes ATAM (Architecture Tradeoff Analysis Method) [Kazman, Klein, Barbacci, Longstaff, Lipson and Carriere, 1998; Kazman, Klein and Clements, 2000; Bass et al., 2002; Clements et al., 2002], SAAM (Software Architecture Analysis Method) [Kazman, Bass, Webb and Abowd, 1994; Kazman, Abowd, Bass and Clements, 1996; Clements et al., 2002], ARID (Active Reviews for Intermediate Design) [Clements et al., 2002], SPE (Software Performance Engineering) [Smith, 1990], and ADR (Active Design Reviews) [Parnas and Weiss, 1985]. However, there are yet to be similar assessment methods for product line architectures.

The assessment of product line architectures is significantly more complex and none of the current generation of architecture assessment methods provide a comprehensive assessment of the software architecture in a product line context. There are two main goals that motivated the research reported in this book. One of them was to investigate some of the characteristics of product line architectures that make their assessment peculiar. We particularly focus investigations on understanding how the need to make reuse more flexible can impact the quality attributes of individual products in a product line. Our second goal was to use the result of the investigations as the conceptual basis for developing a suitable assessment method for product line architectures. we realised both goals in the course of the research. The latter goal eventually led to the creation of a new assessment method called Holistic Product Line Architecture Assessment (HoPLAA) . HoPLAA is an extension of the ATAM method for product line architectures assessment. The ATAM is one of the most widely used architecture evaluation methods.

In the remainder of this chapter, we will describe what a software architecture is, as well as its importance in modern software development. Following that, we will introduce the concept of software product lines and present some of the challenges that make product line architecture (PLA) assessment more difficult and complex, compared with single product architecture (SPA) assessment. Finally, we will highlight the main contributions of the book, and outline the organization of its remaining parts.

1.2 Software architecture

There are over 50 definitions of software architecture, out of which we present the two most commonly used ones. The first is by the ANSI/IEEE Std 1471-2000 Recommended Practice for Architectural Description of Software-Intensive Systems [IEEE, 2000] and it states:

> *Architecture is defined by the recommended practice as the fundamental organization of a system, embodied in its components, their relationships to each other and the environment, and the principles governing its design and evolution.*

The second definition is given by the Carnegie Mellon University Software Engineering Institute (SEI) [Bass et al., 2002]:

> *The software architecture of a program or computing system is the structure or structures of the system, which comprise software elements, the externally visible properties of those elements, and the relationships among them.*

The two definitions present the architecture of a software-intensive system as an abstraction of the system which consists of various computational units, their interrelationship or interactions and some rules guiding these interactions. The computational units are essentially black-boxes as the internal properties of components are not considered in an architectural abstraction.

The architecture plays several significant roles in the development of large software-intensive systems [Clements et al., 2002]

- Architecture is the earliest representation of the high level software system design that ultimately determines the quality attribute responses of the implemented system. For instance, if performance and security are important quality attribute goals of a software system, the architecture is the first place to begin to determine that the eventual solution could in fact meet these goals.

- Architecture provides a blueprint from which the detailed design can proceed, and which will eventually be materialised in the actual software system.

- Architecture provides an effective vehicle for reasoning about the system before it is actually built. As such, it provides the means for communicating a software design to development team members and other stakeholders alike. This is possible because an architectural abstraction can be presented in different views to suit a particular audience - technical or non-technical stakeholders. The views are useful for understanding the system's blueprint and to create work assignments, schedule and budget.

- Finally, an architectural abstraction can be reused between software systems exhibiting similar requirements. Since architecture definition is a crucial, costly and time consuming exercise, it makes perfect sense to reuse it so that the cost of development can be spread over several development projects.

These are just some of the reasons why several organizations are capitalizing on the architecture for developing ranges of similar products using the software product line approach.

1.3   Software product lines

The idea of applying the product line concept to software development originates from Parnas in 1978, when he noted that [Parnas, 1978]: 'we consider a set of programs to be a program family if they have so much in common that it pays to study their common aspects before looking at the aspects that differentiate them.' The reuse of development effort and knowledge to achieve improved product quality, faster time-to-market, and reduced cost, are the key motivation for the product line approach to software development [Bass et al., 2002; Bosch, 2000; Clements and Northrop, 2002].

As mentioned above, the software product line or product family can be defined as a set of programs developed in a systematic way from a common architecture and a set of reusable components in order to satisfy the needs of a set of related yet distinct market segments [Clements and Northrop, 2002].

Organizations that develop software product lines generally follow one of the two main adoption approaches, which are often referred to as *revolutionary* and *evolutionary* [Bosch, 2000]. In the revolutionary approach, the common architecture and some set of reusable components are first developed before the development of the first product. These components are then combined as necessary in order to obtain the individual products in the family.

For the evolutionary approach, the common architecture (and sometimes, the set of reusable components) is typically developed from existing products and/or legacy artifacts. That is, product development evolves or goes along with the creation of architectural artefacts. The development of the first product can proceed simultaneously as changes are being made in the common architecture. Industrial experiences have shown that the evolutionary approach is a more popular path of adopting the product line concept [Bosch, 2002; Simon and Eisenbarth, 2002; Staples and Hill, 2004].

During the product line development, requirements (or features) that cut across to all the products, called *commonalities*, are specified into a common *core architecture* (CA), while the requirements that are specific to some, but not all the products, called *variability*, are represented as *variation points* in the CA. Individual products are subsequently developed from the CA, by replacing the variation points with product-specific component instances, called *variants*. In some cases, individual products are not developed directly from the CA, but are developed instead from separate architectures, called the individual *product architectures* (PA). Individual PAs are created from the CA by exercising the built-in variation points. This *dual form* of representation of the architecture (i.e., CA and PA) is typical of the software product lines [Bosch, 2000; Clements and Northrop, 2002; Clements and Northrop, 2005].

1.4 Problems of product line architectures assessment

The PLAs possess some characteristics that make the development and assessment of such architectures difficult. A number of development methods for such architectures have been proposed, as well as a (much smaller) number of assessment methods. However, most of the assessment methods proposed are oriented towards SPAs and do not take due cognisance of the peculiarities of the PLA.

The assessment of PLAs is significantly more complex than the assessment of SPAs. An initial understanding of this complexity can be obtained by considering the inherently interacting and possibly conflicting motives behind the quality specification of the CA and the subsequent definitions of the PAs. The CA is fully specified to fulfill functional and quality goals common to all products. At the same time, it is underspecified at the points of variability to cater to the specifics of the PAs. This room for flexibility towards PAs creation oftentimes result in conflict between the quality attributes that are exhibited by the CA and PAs.

The problem of assessing product line architectures needs an approach that considers not only the quality attributes common to the family of systems, but also those specific to some members only, and their interrelationships. It should be noted that individual PAs may require a different prioritization of the quality goals common to the PLA, and they may even be associated with quality goals which are not present in other members of the product line.

Next, we present some of characteristics of the PLAs and the attendant research questions not answered by the current generation of architecture assessment methods.

The dual form of the architecture: Since the architecture assumes a dual form [Clements and Northrop, 2002] in the product line, the priorities of the requirements and (oftentimes) the requirements themselves usually differ from the CA to the PA. This is quite unlike single product architectures where the requirements are prioritized in a simple, single list.

Question: How can we tailor an assessment method to deal with the two types of architectures in a product line context - the CA and individual PAs? Will such specialised evaluation treatment of the common CA and the PAs be an improvement over the one-size-fit-all approach of existing architecture assessment methods?

The presence of variation points in the CA: The CA provides explicit support for variability using variation points. The PA augments the CA with additional functional and quality requirements in those areas (i.e., the variation points). Variation points now need to be analyzed for the quality attribute requirements.

Question: Now that architectural variations are planned for in the CA (unlike single product architectures where changes are usually unplanned for or unknown), what impact will variation points have on software quality and how can they be analyzed?

Quality attributes scenarios are more complex to deal with: Most assessment methods analyze architectures using a short story involving a user interaction with the program, called *scenarios*. Scenario-based methods are perfectly fit for a risk-mitigating evaluation because the program to be evaluated may not yet exist (i.e., not finished) [Clements et al., 2002]. It is now possible to associate analysis context with more scenarios than may be the case with a SPAs. In particular, quality attributes scenarios take three forms in a product line evaluation - mandatory, alternative, and optional. The mandatory scenarios apply to all products, and should be isolated for the CA analysis. The alternative and optional scenarios are product-specific and should only apply to the analysis of individual PAs.

Question: Scenarios in a product line architecture evaluation are context-dependent (i.e., applies either to the core PLA or to one or more individual PAs) and are significantly more in numbers (several hundreds - since several products are involved). Is there a way to simplify the process of scenarios generation, prioritization and analysis?

Quality attribute interactions: Quality attribute interactions is an important aspect of architecture assessment because they make visible to software architects or developers the areas of the architecture that pose the greatest risks. This interaction can be classified as sensitivities and tradeoffs. Areas of the architecture whose design decisions have the potential of determining one or more quality attributes are called *sensitivity points*. An area of the architecture whose design decisions is a sensitivity point for two or more (possibly conflicting) quality attributes is called a *tradeoff point*. Some of the existing architecture assessment methods permit analysis of architectural decisions that produce sensitivities and tradeoffs within the same architecture. For example, architectural design decision that improve security by encrypting message exchange between components will similarly degrade performance to some extent (due to the time required for the encryption/decryption of messages by components). In a product line context, quality attributes interact within a single PA or the CA. In addition, interactions exist between the quality attributes of the PA in relation to the CA by virtue of the effects of the design decisions of the PA on earlier decisions in the CA.

Question: Now that two types of related architectures are considered, how can this analysis be extended to quality interactions across architectures as opposed to a single architecture? The rationale for this is the dependence of all of a product line's PAs on design decisions previously made in the CA. We will use the term *horizontal* to qualify sensitivities and tradeoffs in quality attributes within a single architecture (the CA or a PA). Similarly, we will use the term *vertical* to qualify sensitivities and tradeoffs in quality attributes across two or more architectures (the CA and the PAs). Horizontal sensitivities occur when an architecture's response to one or more quality attributes depends on design decision(s) localized on that architecture alone. That is, such design decisions are independent of any prior decisions. This is the usual type of sensitivities introduced by the ATAM. Going forward, vertical sensitivities occur when an architecture's response to one or more quality attributes is not only dependent on design decisions of that architecture, but also on prior decisions that has been made on some aspects of the design. This form of sensitivity typically applies in a PLA wherein the design decisions of a PA are influenced by prior decisions of the CA.

Finally, the assessment of individual PAs must be such that it optimally reuses prior and relevant results produced from the PLA evaluation. None of these characteristics are addressed by the currently existing methods. This shortcoming justifies the need for an architecture evaluation method specifically tailored to address the requirements of software product line architectures.

1.5 Contributions of this book

The research reported in this book contributes to the field of software engineering, and in particular the architecture and product line community, in the following ways:

- First, to the best of our knowledge and from available publications, this work is the first that provides assessment-focused characterization of the dual forms of architectures in product lines. This research explored the characterization of the relationship between variation points and quality attributes as the shape of the architecture is defined by the design decisions of the CA and the PA. This characterization helps in the understanding and development of suitable assessment methods for PLAs.

- Second, this research produces an architecture-centric, risk-mitigating assessment method for software product lines. There is currently no assessment method that is oriented to software product lines in this manner. The assessment method developed in this research, called HoPLAA (Holistic Product Line Architecture Assessment), is suitable for assessing both fresh PLAs undergoing development and existing PLA designs. It can also be used for comparing two or more PLA design alternatives and in situations where limited manpower is available to conduct the PLA assessment.

- Finally, this work develops a quality attribute conformance checking technique for ensuring that the quality attributes designed for in the CA are not inadvertently eroded by the design decisions of the PA. This is important for the development and evolution of a product line because it is always desired that the PAs remains in quality conformance with the CA. Any inconsistencies tend to complicate maintenance activities. This technique is based on the concept of variation points . The conformance checking technique is suitable for product line developed using either the evolutionary approach or revolutionary approach. Further, following this technique in a product line development ensures the as-designed (or documented) architecture of a product line always remain in quality congruence with the as-built (or running) architecture.

2

Related Work

In this chapter, we will explain some areas of software architecture and software product line research that relate to this book. In the first section, we will review related research on software architecture in general, how it came to be, the development of the architecture concept, its representation with views, and its quality. The second section will describe the concept of product line architecture, while the third section will focus on existing methods and techniques used for architecture assessment in general. The last section will focus on the research related to product line architecture assessment.

2.1 Architecture

Research on software architecture began in the late 1960s when Edsger Dijkstra [Dijkstra, 1968] noted that programmers should consider how to structure a computer program in addition to making it compute correctly. Despite this insight, books that provide expositional coverage on software architecture did not become available until recently (e.g., [Bass et al., 2002; Hofmeister, Nord and Soni, 1999; Bosch, 2000; Malveau, 2000; Shaw and Garlan, 1996]).

The IEEE Standard 1061 [Staff, 1998] defines software quality as the extent 'to which software possesses a desired combination of quality attributes'. These quality attributes or qualities are defined by another standard, the ISO/IEC Draft 9216-1 [ISO/IEC, 2001] to be functionality, reliability, usability, efficiency, maintainability, and portability. Each of these six attributes are further refined into a number of sub-characteristics, which are sometimes called *attribute concerns* [Clements et al., 2002; Barbacci, Clements, Lattanze, Northrop and Wood, 2003]. An attribute concern is an aspect of a quality attribute that is of primary concern in the assessment of a particular software system. Software quality attributes are not limited to the six attributes defined by the ISO/IEC Draft 9216-1. Bass et al. [Bass et al., 2002] provides a more elaborate, but open ended list of quality attributes. The work recommends as a potential quality attribute any word ending with 'illities' in the requirements documentation. It also classifies quality attributes into two broad categories - execution and evolution. Execution qualities are expressed by the behavior of the system at runtime. On the other hand, evolution qualities reside in the static structure of the software system (e.g., architecture).

The idea to use the architecture as the high-level design vehicle for software quality prediction originates from Parnas in a 1972 seminal paper [Parnas, 1972]. He proposed modularity and information hiding as means of enhancing program flexibility and system comprehension. Boehm et. al.[Boehm, Brown and Lipow, 1976] further helped establish a conceptual framework that clarifies the understanding of qualitative analysis of the architecture using a set of definitions and experiences. The architecture research group at the Software Engineering Institute (SEI) affiliated with Carnegie Mellon University in Pittsburgh, PA (USA), introduced the concept of an *architecture business cycle* that traces software quality attributes to the business goal of an organization [Bass et al., 2002]. This enables architecture analysis only with respect to those quality attribute goals which are traceable from the organizations business goal. In a way, there is a two-way relationship: the business impacts the architecture whilst the architecture, through its eventual materialization as software, impact the business by its quality attributes. Several software development processes (e.g., MDA [OMG, 2003], RUP [Kazman, Kruchten, Nord and Tomayko, 2004; RUP, 2001]) now provide guidance for including architecture analysis as part of their respective life cycle models.

However, knowing the qualities desired of a software system is not enough. There is also the problem of defining (or developing) the architecture to fulfill those quality goals. This problem has been addressed through the use of architectural *styles* [Shaw and Garlan, 1996] and design *tactics* [Bachmann, Bass and Klein, 2003a; Bass et al., 2002]. While an architectural style defines known component topology in terms of how they interact and their runtime quality, the tactics are a collection of design decisions that are used to achieve specific quality attribute responses. For example, redundancy tactics is used to achieve high availability. Tactics and architectural styles are not complete architectures, but rather aids that facilitate the development of the architecture and its constituent parts. Shaw and Garlan [Shaw and Garlan, 1996] provide a comprehensive catalogue of architectural styles or idioms. An updated collection of such styles with a closer tie to software quality, termed tactics, has been developed by the SEI [Bass et al., 2002].

The architecture, once defined, is documented as a collection of views. A *view* 'is a coherent representation of a set of architectural elements' [Bass et al., 2002]. A view is perhaps best understood by analogy to the similar concept used in a building plan, where a number of views such as a pipeline diagram, electrical diagram, room layout, and others, depict the building from different angles. Kruchten's [Kruchten, 1995] 4+1 model on software architectural views expresses five separate views of the architecture: logical, process (or concurrency), physical, development (or implementation), and use cases (or scenarios) views. A modernised view classification in [Clements et al., 2002] includes functional, process (or concurrency), code, development (or implementation) and process.

The use of separate architectural views is important on two counts. First, it enables separation of concerns – i.e., specific interests of different stakeholders: end-users, developers, and managers, among others. For example, end-users will find the code view completely meaningless, whereas this view is most appropriate for the programmers. Second, it helps in software quality assessment. For example, a process (or concurrency) view of an architecture is popularly used for studying the performance quality.

Two other terms closely related to the description of architectural views are *viewpoints* and *perspectives* . According to the ANSI/IEEE Std 1471-2000 [IEEE, 2000], a view documents some aspects of an architecture based on some concerns held by one or more stakeholders. A viewpoint specifies the stakeholders of a view along with some guidelines for constructing the structure of that view. A viewpoint has to do with specified knowledge about creating an architectural structure; which is more or less functional or behavioural structures. This concept is extended to deal with the quality attribute of an architecture in [Woods and Rozanski, 2005], instead of functional aspects. They used the term architectural perspective for this. According to the authors, an architectural perspective provides a means of designing the architecture to fulfill some quality using a number of views [Woods and Rozanski, 2005]. More than one view is needed because the nature of most quality attributes is best understood using different views.

The most useful and precise architectural descriptions are formalized into a modelling language; such languages are known as architecture description languages (ADL). The ADL model of an architecture can be subject to mathematical analysis using appropriate formalisms and tools. Some of the ADLs and the accompanying tool in use in software architecture community are ACME, Rapide, Darwin, xADL 2.0, ArchStudio, Aesop and ArgoUML [Dashofy, der Hoek and Taylor, 2001]. The xADL 2.0 which is based on xADL, provides an XML description of an architecture which can be easily converted to proprietary representations used in other ADL environments. xADL is a standard XML-based representation for software architectures [Khare, Guntersdorfer, Oreizy, Medvidovic and Taylor, 2001; Dashofy et al., 2001]. The Wright and Darwin ADLs [Dashofy et al., 2001] are focused on formally specifying the architecture description of a system to eliminate ambiguity and guarantee appropriate quality attributes. Wright is based on process algebra. Darwin is based on pi calculus [Magee, Dulay, Eisenbach and Kramer, 1995; Giannakopoulou and Magee, 2003]. UML is the popular industry standard for architectural documentation of developer and the user views. According to Medvidovic et al. [Medvidovic, Rosenblum, Redmiles and Robbins, 2002], UML lacks the required formal grounding to specify certain architectural concerns such as an explicit modeling of connectors, and local and global architectural constraints. The reader should recall that a connector is an architectural element that mediates interactions between two or more components. A comparison of conventional ADLs is available in [Medvidovic and Taylor, 1997]. While the UML enjoys popular usage in the industry, most academic researchers favour the use of formal ADLs [Medvidovic and Taylor, 1997; Medvidovic and Taylor, 2000; Garlan, Monroe and Wile, 1997].

Despite the importance of software architecture, it is common for some systems to be developed without an architecture. Also, the documentation of the architecture may be lost, or become outdated. The architecture documentation may not accurately reflect the true state of the system or its runtime image, especially from its observable qualities. For example, an architecture may have become very complex and difficult to maintain further as a result of some series of hastily planned updates. For such systems, the architecture can be reconstructed from the existing programs through a process called *reverse engineering* or *re-engineering* or . Several techniques for reverse engineering have been proposed. For example Hassan et al. [Hassan and Holt, 2000] explain how human knowledge, available documentation and source code can assist in architecture reconstruction.

Architectural reconstruction requires the use of tools; as most tools are either language-biased (e.g., Java, C, C++, Ada) or operating system dependent, there cannot be a single comprehensive architecture reconstruction tool. Example of such tools are ARIS [Mitchell, Mancoridis and Traverso, 2002], Dali [Kazman and Carriëre, 1999]. Re-engineering techniques are also being used to develop the product line architecture (the CA) from existing system and legacy artifacts [Olumofin and Vojislav B. Mišić , 2005*b*].

The architecture plays an important role in virtually every phase of a software development cycle. Quality attributes, as opposed to functional properties are what largely determine the shape of the architecture. Having a right architecture that will guarantee the quality requirements of an end system is therefore a recipe for success. This is even more true for a product line where many products are staked on the architecture. The architecture must therefore be assessed to safeguard resources already invested and the intended system or family of systems to be built from it.

2.2   Product lines

Reuse has long been identified for its great potential for improving software development productivity [Clements et al., 2002; Jazayeri, Ran and van der Linden, 2000]. Right from the early days of subroutines and module libraries to components and domain specific architectures, the concept of software reuse has been steadily gaining importance. As the granularity or size of reuse increases, the benefits of reuse become more real. However, none of these earlier forms of reuse compares to the benefit accruable from large-scale architecture reuse based on the product line approach to software development.

Software product line offers the greatest promise of maximising the benefits of reuse. The reuse is first planned before it is exploited. The reused artifacts are called *core assets* and include requirements documents, software architecture, components, test cases, schedule, budget and so on. The core assets are developed so that it may be reused in more than one product. Substantial cost is saved from the product line approach because the artifacts constituting the core assets are oftentimes the most difficult to develop in any software development project. The advantage of economies of scale comes into play here. It is generally held in industry that the product line development pays off with as few as four to six products [Weiss and Lai, 1999].

However, for the product line approach to be successful in any organization, there are some technical and non-technical factors that need to be considered. The SEI identifies core asset development and product development as two essential technical practice areas [Clements and Northrop, 2005; Clements and Northrop, 2002]. The process of core assets creation is sometimes called *domain engineering*. It entails setting the scope for the products, developing the architecture and the other artifacts that will be used as the basis of creating individual products, and creating the description of the way in which the products will be created from the core assets. Product development exploits the core assets by substituting existing variations with aspects related to the requirements of a particular product. This process is sometimes called *application engineering*. The non-technical or managerial aspects include both technical (or project) management and organizational management. Technical management is vital for the creation of the core assets for example. Organizational management provides the right organizational structures to support the mission of the particular product line. This may involve creation of new personnel roles like product line developer, core asset maintainer and so on [Clements and Northrop, 2002] to support the new work roles required by product line development.

A similar classification of the technical and non-technical factors affecting the success of the product line approach comes about from the European efforts in family engineering like the Information Technology for European Advancement (ITEA) projects if9005 ESAPS (1999-2001), if00004 CAF (2001-2003), and if02009 FAM-ILIES (2003-2005) [van der Linden, Bosch, Kamsties, Känsälä and Obbink, 2004]. It identifies four interrelated engineering concerns, which are business, architecture, organization and process. Only the architecture is purely technical, while the rest are non-technical issues. In addition, the business concerns are the economic benefits of the product family initiative. The architecture, which must reflect business goals, concerns the technical means for realising the products in the family. The process concerns are the steps to follow within a development organization in building the products specified by the architecture. The organization concern is the mapping of process to organizational structures [Bosch, 2002; van der Linden, Bosch, Kamsties, Känsälä, Krzanik and Obbink, 2003].

The development of the product line architecture (PLA) is at the core of the technical practice area. A PLA is more challenging to define than a SPA, for obvious reasons. A PLA captures the commonality of the product line and equality provides built-in mechanism for variations. The fact that individual products may require widely different and sometimes even conflicting functional and quality attributes, makes this task all the more challenging. The PLA development must also specify the mechanism for achieving variability, which may use a number of different mechanisms such as inheritance, extension points, parameterization, configuration and module interconnection languages, and compile time directives [Svahnberg and Bosch, 2000]. Existing SPA development techniques such as the use of architectural styles and patterns, are equally useful.

Matinlassi [Matinlassi, 2004] carried out a study that compared five of the existing PLA design methods: COPA, FAST, FORM, KobrA and QADA. The concepts underlying each method were found to be very distinct, even though they are all aimed at solving the same problem: the PLA design. COPA is a comprehensive method for

PLA development. It is architecture centric and equally supports non-technical managerial issues. FAST is an adaptable process for product line development. FORM is suited for capturing commonalities or mandatory features to use for creating the PLA. The KobrA method was developed by the Fraunhofer IESE, as a component-based method for modeling both SPA and PLAs. QADA is oriented towards the development and assessment of PLAs to satisfy quality goals[Matinlassi, 2004].

The PLA can be used in one of two ways for creating individual products. It can be used directly to create individual products (in which case it takes the form of the CA) or it can be specialized to a product architecture (i.e., PA) and have individual product built from this architecture. The single architecture approach is appropriate for relatively small product lines where the functional and quality requirements of individual products are very similar. The multi-architecture approach applies to medium and large product lines with complex requirements.

2.3 SPA assessment

The understanding that the quality attributes of a large software system are principally determined by the underlying architecture, provides the foundation for the development of several architecture assessment methods. In this section, we will briefly describe some of the existing SPA assessment methods.

2.3.1 Software Architecture Analysis Method (SAAM)

The Software Architecture Analysis Method (SAAM), developed by SEI, is one of the first and widely publicized SPA assessment methods [Clements et al., 2002]. The SAAM involves a practical process for verifying or testing claims of fitness or quality (including modifiability, maintainability, and the like) made by practitioners of software architecture about their systems [Clements et al., 2002; Kazman et al., 1994]. Originally, SAAM was used only for the assessment of modifiability in its various forms. Nevertheless, experience shows it is suitable for evaluating competing architectural solutions for other quality attributes like performance, functionality, portability, extensibility, and integrability [Clements et al., 2002; Kazman et al., 1996].

The SAAM employs scenarios to elicit a representation of the architecture and derive quality attribute goals for the analysis. A *scenario* is a concise description of the interaction of one of the stakeholders with the system. Usually, a complete scenario is structured in a three-part format: stimulus, environment, and response [Clements et al., 2002]. The *stimulus* describes the action initiated by the stakeholder to interact with the system. The *environment* describes the systems state prior to the stimulus. The *response* explains how the architecture of the system should respond to the stimulus. Kazman et al.[Kazman et al., 1996] classified scenarios as direct and indirect for the purpose of SAAM evaluation. *Direct scenarios* are those that

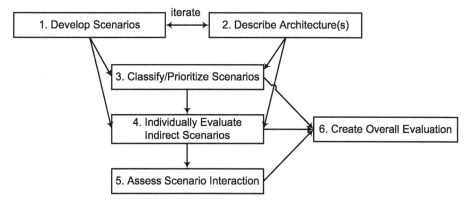

FIGURE 2.1
Activities and dependencies in a SAAM evaluation (Clements et al., 2002).

the architecture can satisfy (i.e., the architecture response is as expected). *Indirect scenarios* are those that require modifications to the architecture before they can be satisfied.

The prescribed steps for SAAM evaluation are illustrated in Figure 2.1. These steps are preceded by a brief presentation of the architecture and its business goals.

Step 1: Scenario development

The SAAM evaluation must comprise scenarios that elicit immediate and future functional and quality requirements from the perspective of all stakeholders (or users) of the system. The scenario generation process is iterative and involves brainstorming. This step is closely related to the architecture description step (i.e., step 2).

Step 2: Architecture description

The architecture(s) under consideration must be clearly described in a notation comprehensible to the stakeholders. This description must explicitly identify the components or computation unit, connectors that mediate data and control flows, as well as interdependencies among the components.

Step 3: Scenario classification and prioritization

The scenarios identified are classified as either direct or indirect. While direct scenarios improve understanding of the architecture(s) under evaluation, indirect scenarios illuminate functional and quality goals that are not currently satisfied but could become important requirements in the future. The classified scenarios, for the reason of limited time for the evaluation, are also prioritized in their order of importance to the stakeholders.

Step 4: Evaluation of indirect scenarios

The direct scenarios are evaluated with a demonstration of how the architecture supports them. Also, the most important indirect scenarios are individually evaluated with regard to the architecture to ascertain what changes are needed and the cost of efforts for making them to the architecture. The end product of this step is a summary table that lists all scenarios and the modifications needed in the case of indirect scenarios.

Step 5: Assessment of scenario interactions

Whenever two indirect scenarios require modifications to the same component or connector, they are said to *interact* in that component or connector. The assessment of indirect scenarios interactions is important on two counts. First, it identifies areas of inadequate separation of concerns or structural complexity. This will be the case whenever two semantically unrelated components interact. Second, it highlights components that are not in the appropriate level of structural decomposition. For such components, splitting them into sub-components may be the required architectural task to address such scenario interaction.

Step 6: Overall evaluation

Finally, weights are assigned to each scenario based on its relative importance to the overall system goals. The process of weight determination for each scenario is subjective and best achieved when interests of every stakeholder are considered. The weights are useful in determining overall ranking, in particular if a SAAM evaluation involves the comparison of two or more candidate architectures.

Apart from the generic risk mitigation advantage of architecture evaluation, a SAAM evaluation provides two important benefits. First, it leads to improved documentation of the architecture. Of note is the treatment of the indirect scenarios which provides guidance on how the architecture can evolve or how it can support a family of related systems. The second benefit is social, that is, the facilitation of shared understanding of the architecture amongst participating stakeholders. A typical SAAM evaluation can be carried out by two persons [Clements et al., 2002].

2.3.2   Architecture Tradeoff Analysis Method (ATAM)

The ATAM is the successor of the SAAM and it is suitable for analysing multiple quality attributes. It helps identify the architectural approaches used and, by means of scenarios, exposes areas of risk as a result. It can also be used for the tradeoff analysis assessment of areas of the architecture in which the response of two or more quality attributes are determined by a single design decision. The ATAM is made up of nine steps. An ATAM evaluation of a SPA produces a number of outputs including a list of architectural approaches, a list of most important requirements, a scenarios list, areas of risk, sensitivities and tradeoffs. A more detailed description of the ATAM will be presented in Section 3.1. A number of detailed examples of the use of ATAM can be found in [Clements et al., 2002].

2.3.3   Active Reviews for Intermediate Design (ARID)

The ARID [Clements et al., 2002] is a scenario-based assessment method developed by the SEI for evaluating intermediate designs or parts of an architecture. An ARID assessment is usually carried out to confirm if the design of a part of the architecture is suitable for its intended purpose before it has been fully documented. It is based on the ATAM and the work on active design reviews (ADRs) by Parnas [Parnas and Weiss, 1985]. ARID has nine steps just like the ATAM, and they are completed in two phases: rehearsal and review. The steps are reviewer's identification, design briefing preparation, seed scenario preparation, material preparation, ARID presentation, design presentation, scenarios brainstorm and prioritization, scenarios application and summary production. The first four of these steps are in Phase 1, while the rest are in Phase 2.

2.3.4   Cost Benefit Analysis Method (CBAM)

Architecture analysis can be based on the economic aspects of the costs and benefits of architectural decisions. Using the work of Barry Boehm [Boehm, 1981], the originator of software architecture economics, and others, the architecture group at SEI has developed the CBAM (Cost Benefit Analysis Method) [Kazman, Asundi and Klein, 2002; Nord, Barbacci, Clements, Kazman, Klein, O'Brien and Tomayko, 2003]. The CBAM enhances the Boehm economic model to include not only the cost of architectural decisions, but also the benefits aspect [Nord et al., 2003].

2.4   PLA assessment

In a product line, the common or core architecture (CA) captures the common requirements (or commonalities) of the products and represents varying requirements (or variability) using the variation points. Individual products are subsequently built on the basis of both common and product-specific requirements. This is accomplished either by extending the PLA through direct addition of components, or by modifying the PLA to obtain the individual product architectures (PAs), and then building the products from the respective PAs. In the first approach, products are developed from a single, common architecture, while in the second approach, products have architectures of their own.

The first approach ignores the individual PAs by having products developed directly from the common architecture. To evaluate this CA, it might seem that any suitable single product architecture evaluation method would suffice, since there is only a single architecture to deal with. The problem with this approach lies in the fact that the core architecture allows only the quality attributes common to all products, while those attributes specific to a single product only or to some (but not all) of them, are not taken into account at all. At best, a separate evaluation of architectures of individual products (which were not defined in the first place) would be needed. Needless to say, this is a time consuming and not very useful exercise, at best. Furthermore, the simplified, single-architecture approach cannot be applied to large, complex product lines in which the characteristics of individual products differ widely from one product to another.

The range of available SPA evaluation methods that can be used for analysing the CA developed following the single architecture, many products approach includes the SAAM [Kazman et al., 1996; Kazman et al., 1994], the ATAM [Bass et al., 2002; Clements et al., 2002; Kazman et al., 2000], and ARID [Clements et al., 2002]. All of these SPA methods use scenarios as the vehicle both for describing and analyzing software architectures. (Scenarios and other questioning techniques, such as questionnaires and checklists, are well suited to architectural evaluation because no running system is necessary [Clements et al., 2002].) Among those, ATAM is probably the most widely used. It was the first to introduce the concept of tradeoff analysis between two or more quality attributes. Furthermore, it has been successfully applied to the evaluation of product line architectures [Barbacci et al., 2003]. However, the PLA in question used the single-architecture approach mentioned above. That is, a small or medium product line wherein the characteristics of individual products does not differ very widely. The second architecture evaluation approach is the measuring technique which is based on the use of metrics. For example, the use of a performance metric to simulate an architecture's performance at peak workload profile.

The problems of the first approach are addressed by the alternative approach that recognizes the dual form of the product line architectures [Clements and Northrop, 2002; Clements and Northrop, 2005]. The PLA covers the common features, while individual PAs pertain to the requirements specific to individual products; both of these need to be evaluated [Clements and Northrop, 2002]. While some steps have been taken to make use of that context, the results are far from being satisfactory.

2.4.1   Product Line Software Engineering - Domain-Specific Software Architecture (PuLSE-DSSA)

PuLSE-DSSA (Product Line Software Engineering - Domain-Specific Software Architecture) is the evaluation-focused component of the PuLSE [DeBaud, Flege and Knauber, 1998] methodology for the iterative creation and evaluation of reference architectures [Bayer, Anastasopoulos, Gacek and Flege, 2000]. However, it has limited applicability as the evaluation process is bound to the PuLSE methodology. Further, there is no tradeoff analysis as it iteratively defines evaluation criteria per scenario. However, it claims to have the capability for regression evaluation [DeBaud et al., 1998; Bayer et al., 2000].

2.4.2 VTT PLA evaluation framework

An iterative PLA evaluation framework has been developed by the Valtion Teknilli-nen Tutkimuskeskus (VTT) Technical Research Centre of Finland (VTT TRC) [Dobrica and Niemelä, 2000]. It uses the measurement instrument 'defined by a taxonomy' for quality attributes, which are organized with respect to three main elements: qual-ity attribute priority, architecture view, and analysis method [Dobrica and Niemelä, 2000]. For example, [performance, process view, ATAM] describes the evaluation of the process view of an architecture for performance, using the ATAM evaluation method [Dobrica and Niemelä, 2000]. The VTT TRC framework is fairly flexible, as it can leverage the advantages of several other architecture evaluation methods, and has a definite product line focus. However, it does rely on both evaluators and developers possessing good skills with different methods and, thus, constitute a steep learning curve.

2.4.3 Family Evaluation Framework (FEF)

The product line engineering capability of an organization is addressed through the European ITEA projects. The resulting Family Evaluation Framework (FEF) is a four-dimensional framework of business, architecture, process, and organization [Niemelä, Matinlassi and Taulavuori, 2004; van der Linden et al., 2004]. The FEF is useful for benchmarking the product line engineering capability (or maturity) of an organization, analogous to the well known SEI Capability Maturity Model In-tegration framework [Chrissis, Konrad and Shrum, 2003]. Despite its treatment of architecture concerns, it is not architecture-centric and cannot serve the purpose of a risk-mitigating architectural evaluation exercise. Besides, its architecture dimension only applies to architectures of existing systems, which essentially renders it useless for the evaluation of PLAs under development.

2.4.4 Assessing architecture analysis methods

Research on architecture assessment methodology in the past decade has produced a good number of architecture analysis methods. Unfortunately, this availability of varieties also create a new problem; that of selecting which method is best for assessing an architecture for which a number of different quality goals are important. Selection is important because each of these methods follows their own unique idea, concepts and techniques.

A very early work on methodology assessment is the NIMSAD (Normative Infor-mation Model-Based Systems Analysis and Design) [Jayaratna, 1994]. The NIM-SAD is a well known and authoritative reference for creating an evaluation frame-work for methodologies. Already, there are two NIMSAD-oriented comparison frameworks that attempt to taxonomize some of the existing SPA assessment meth-ods using a number of criteria [Dobrica and Niemelä, 2002; Babar and Gorton, 2004]. According to Kazman et al [Kazman, Bass, Klein, Lattanze and Northrop, 2005], the criteria suggested by these two work are based on the features of the method rather than the essence of what an analysis method should be. In its place, they proposed four criteria for evaluating an architecture analysis method and for comparing two or more methods. These criteria essentially assess how effective and usable an analysis method is. In their context, effective means how reliable a method is to produce result in a repeatable and predictable manner. Whereas, usable refers to how easy it is to learn, understand, and apply a method in a cost effective way. The four criteria are [Kazman et al., 2005]:

Context and goal: How are context and goals identified and recorded? The goals are the quality attribute for the analysis. Context of the analysis include the state of the architecture which may be early (prior to coding) or late (e.g., architecture of existing system). Constraints on the architecture such as using a particular platform or operating system also form part of the context for the analysis.

Focus and properties under examination: How does the method focus analysis efforts on specific areas of the architecture interacting with the quality goals? Are there means of finding and mitigating technical risks associated with these quality goals? Also, the method should help analysts maintain focus on the objectives of the analysis and not drift away to other important aspects of a project such as complaints about schedules, funding, or even management.

Analysis support: What supporting materials and aids does the method offer to facilitate repeatable analysis? The support may include templates, techniques, and examples.

Determining analysis outcomes: How does the method guide users to the analysis result and tie this back to the initial analysis goal, in a predictable and repeatable manner?

Since none of the current generation of architecture assessment methods provides adequate coverage for PLA assessment, we are only two options left. The first is to modify an existing SPA assessment method so that it specifically addresses the requirements of software product lines. The second is to create a new PLA assessment method from scratch. Such an extended method, while retaining the well established qualities of SPA assessment methods, should now cater to the dual nature of product line architectures. These notions provide the foundation for the development of the method which will be referred to as the Holistic Product Line Architecture Assessment (HoPLAA) method [Olumofin and Vojislav B. Mišić , 2005a; Olumofin and Mišić, 2007] .

3

HoPLAA: Rationale and main concepts

The development of product line architectures presents significant challenges that may never occur in single product development [Garlan, 2000; Garlan, 2001]. There are two sides to those challenges. On one side, there is the challenge of capturing commonality across multiple products in a single PLA. The commonality includes both functional and quality requirements within the product line scope. On another side, there is the issue of managing varying requirements of product instances as it relates to the product line scope. This is made even more complicated by the fact that individual products may require a different prioritization of the quality goals common to the PLA, and they may even introduce additional quality goals which are not present in other members of the product line.

A comprehensive assessment of product line architectures needs to systematically consider both the common qualities of the product family as well as those that are specific to some products only. The assessment should be systematic in the sense that the relationship between the dual forms of architectures must be exploited to simplify the assessment process.

In the first section of this chapter, we describe one of the SPA assessment methods, ATAM. Following this, we will briefly describe the approach followed to arrive at the solution for the PLA assessment problem. Afterwards, we will present the four concepts or tenets of the solution developed in this research – HoPLAA. These concepts were motivated by the existing SPA assessment methods and existing PLA development methodologies such as the one described in [Kim, Chang and La, 2005]. In particular, we will highlight the concepts borrowed from traditional, single product architecture evaluation methods, as well as the way in which those concepts are adapted to suit the needs of product line architecture evaluation.

We note that the steps of the HoPLAA method, as presented, have undergone a series of revisions in the course of this research. The inputs for the revisions were obtained through the case studies that were used to exercise the method; two of these studies will be described in detail in Chapters 4 and 5.

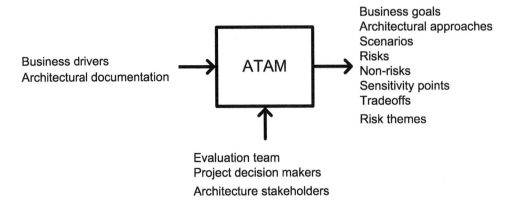

FIGURE 3.1
ATAM inputs, outputs, and participants (From Nord et al., 2003).

3.1   Architecture Tradeoff Analysis Method (ATAM)

The starting point for the development of HoPLAA is the Architecture Tradeoff Analysis Method (ATAM) [Clements et al., 2002; Bass et al., 2002; Barbacci et al., 2003; Nord et al., 2003; Kazman et al., 2000; Kazman et al., 1998]. The ATAM relies on exposing the areas of risks and the way in which design decisions lead to trade-offs between two or more quality attributes in the architecture. Of all scenario-based architecture evaluation methods, ATAM has the best record of successful application in practice [Bass et al., 2002; Barbacci et al., 2003; Clements et al., 2002]. Besides, its trademark feature, the tradeoff analysis between different qualities in a SPA, is not found in other methods. Fig. 3.1 illustrates the inputs, outputs and participants of ATAM.

3.1.1   The steps of ATAM

The ATAM is made up of nine steps that are carried out in four phases: preparation, initial evaluation, complete evaluation, and follow-up. In one step, the activity of phase 0 prepares the team that carries out the evaluation and establishes partnership between them and the sponsor organization. Phases 1 and 2 are the core of the method; they are made up of six and three subsequent steps, respectively. The steps are, in chronological order: present the ATAM, present the business drivers, present the architecture, identify architectural approaches, generate the quality attribute scenarios, analyze architectural approaches, brainstorm and prioritize scenarios, analyze architectural approaches, and present the result. Phase 3 is for follow-up activities like preparation of final reports and documentation.[Clements et al., 2002; Bass et al., 2002; Barbacci et al., 2003; Kazman et al., 1998].

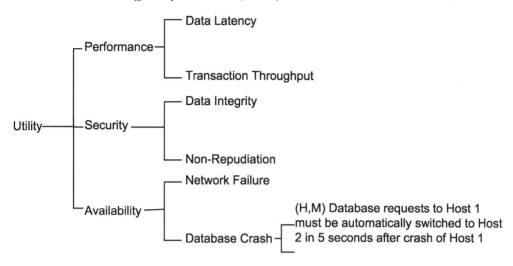

FIGURE 3.2
A sample ATAM utility tree (adapted from Clements et al., 2002).

ATAM represents quality attributes scenarios with a utility tree made up of four levels: Utility, Quality Attribute, Attribute Concern (or Refinement), and Scenarios. The root of the tree is 'Utility' while the leaves are the scenarios. A sample ATAM utility tree is shown in Fig. 3.2. The scenarios in this tree are ranked using the three indexes H, M and L, which stand for High, Medium, and Low respectively. Alternatively, integer values of 3,2, and 1 (or 30, 20, and 10) may be used, respectively.

The scenarios are prioritized according to their weight. The weighting uses the level of importance of the scenario and the level of difficulty of the effort involved in modifying the architecture, to respond appropriately to that scenario. An alternative tabular representation of the utility tree with prioritized scenarios is shown in Table 3.1.

Note that the first level of the tree (i.e., 'Utility') is omitted from the table. The 'Sum' column is the addition of the 'I' and 'D' columns which stand for 'Importance' and 'Difficulty' respectively. The The high-priority scenarios (as determined on the basis of the Sum column) are analyzed to obtain a set of architectural risks, non-risks, sensitivity points, and tradeoff points. For each scenario, a table similar to Table 3.2 is used to document the analysis.

Prefixes AD, R, S, T and NR are Architectural Decisions, Risks, Sensitivity, Tradeoff, and Non-risks, respectively. Each of these references is accompanied by a description like these:

R7. A redundant Host 2 is used as database backup server for the live database in Host 1. The database in Host 2 is updated in near real-time (warm-standby by replication) whenever the live database in Host 1 is updated. It is possible that some uncommitted transactions in the live database are not replicated to

TABLE 3.1
Sample ATAM utility tree.

Level 2:Quality Attribute	Level 3:Attribute Concern	Level 4:Quality Attribute Scenario	I	D	Sum
Security	...	...	...	...	...
Availability	A1:Database Crash	A1.1: Database requests to Host 1 must be automatically switched to Host 2 in 5 seconds after crash of Host 1.	30	20	50
	A2: ...	...	...	...	...
	:	:	:	:	:

TABLE 3.2
Sample ATAM scenario analysis.

Scenario #:A1.1	Database requests to Host 1 must be automatically switched to Host 2 in 5 seconds after crash of Host 1.
Attribute(s)	Availability
Environment	During normal operation
Stimulus	Database goes down in Host 1
Response	Not more than 5 second automatic switchover of requests to Host 2

Architectural Decisions	Risks	Sensitivity	Tradeoff	Non-risks
AD1 Redundant database in Host 2	R7, R8	S1	T3	NR2
:	:	:	:	:
Reasoning				
Architecture Diagram	...			

TABLE 3.3

Scenarios list voting table.

Number	Scenario Description	Votes
1	...	...
:	:	:
100	...	...

the backup before the crash of Host 1. If this is the case, some data may be permanently lost.

S1. Availability of database is sensitive to the type of database redundancy architectural approach adopted.

T3. Improving database availability through redundancy and real-time or near real-time replication may slow down performance.

NR2. Replication requires logging of modification commands submitted by the database management system to the database. This could lead to large disk space requirements for the database log.

During phase 2 of the ATAM, the evaluation team elicit larger (possibly new) set of scenarios and prioritize them by voting. A sample voting table used is shown in Table 3.3.

3.1.2   The ATAM output

An ATAM evaluation produces the following extra outputs: a collection of architectural approaches used, approach and quality attribute analysis questions, sensitivity points, and [*horizontal*] tradeoff points. Other general architecture evaluation outputs produced are: prioritized statement of quality attributes requirements, mapping between architectural approaches and quality attributes, risks and non-risks. Recall that a sensitivity point is a design decision in the architecture that controls the realisation of one or more quality attributes goal. Also, a horizontal tradeoff point (or simply tradeoff point) is a sensitivity point for two or more quality attributes. Note that the horizontal tradeoff point is produced from the usual ATAM-type tradeoff analysis which is limited to a single architecture - the CA or the PA. This is different from the veritcal tradeoff point that is produced from an analysis that extends beyond a single architecture - typically PA analysis in relation to the CA. The ATAM can only be used for horizontal tradeoff analysis.

The transition from Phase 1 to Phase 2 of the ATAM does not always follow consecutively. There could be as much as a two-month interval between the activities of Phase 1 and those of Phase 2 (example [Barbacci et al., 2003]).

3.2   Approaching the problem of PLA assessment

We approached the problem of developing a suitable architecture assessment method
for software product line architectures by considering the existing methods and techniques for SPA assessment, and evaluating their suitability for extension for product
line architecture evaluation.

Of the two main approaches for evaluating software architectures, we selected the
qualitative technique. A qualitative technique does not rely on exact estimates for
the quality assessment of the architecture. For example, it can give an indication
that some design decisions in an architecture being assessed will not produce performance bottlenecks. Exact performance estimates are not required or produced
using this approach. Furthermore, this technique is well suited for both PLA under
development and for assessing related software applications for their potential for
conversion into a product line. The second approach – quantitative techniques– are
largely immature and are meant to complement the result of qualitative techniques
[Babar and Gorton, 2004; Dobrica and Niemelä, 2002; Svahnberg, Wohlin, Lundberg
and Mattsson, 2002]. To date, there are too many issues that are yet to be addressed
with qualitative techniques for architecture assessment.

After exploring the existing generation of assessment methods based on the qualitative technique, we further narrowed down the solution space to the set of scenario-
based architecture assessment methods. Scenario-based assessment methods typically employ short stories about stakeholder interactions with the architecture (or
system) (i.e., scenarios) as the basis for the analysis. It therefore has very little
overhead of application. As long as the number and scope of scenarios used in
exercising the architecture are sufficient, this technique will detect potential problem areas of the architecture (i.e., areas of risk to the achievement of quality goals).
Scenario-based approach to architecture evaluation is the most mature and suitable
for evaluating both the architectures of programs under development and those that
are already running. This is the reason why most of the SPA assessment methods are
essentially scenario-based. Other qualitative techniques (e.g., use of checklists and
questionnaires) are not as widely used.

Although, none of the existing SPA assessment methods is good enough to evaluate PLAs, an ATAM assessment will provide the closest approximation to our desired
PLA assessment. Most existing assessment methods are limited to a single quality
attribute (e.g., SAAM is limited to modifiability), dependent on a specific development methodology (e.g., PuLSE-DSSA), are not architecture-centric (e.g., FEF), or
they simply present a technique for selecting which single product architecture evaluation method is the best to use for analyzing specific quality attributes (e.g., VTT
PLA evaluation framework). The ATAM allows for multiple quality goal assessment and tradeoff analysis. It is a method with several case study validations and
has even been successfully used to assess PLAs developed using the single architecture, many products approach. For this reason, we chose to extend the ATAM into
a new method that addresses the specific requirements of PLA assessment. To that

end, HoPLAA extends the ATAM with the qualitative analytical treatment of variation points and the context-dependent generation, classification, and prioritization of quality attributes scenarios.

In this manner, this research leverages the large body of existing research and industrial experiences in SPA evaluation, while setting the focus on the specific characteristics of software product line architectures.

3.3 The HoPLAA concepts

In this section, we will present the main concepts upon which the HoPLAA approach is built.

3.3.1 Dual-stage assessment steps

The HoPLAA method addresses the requirements for the evaluation of software product line architectures in an integrated, *Holistic approach* with dual-staged, but inter-dependent assessment steps. The main goal of the holistic approach is to simplify the analysis of quality attributes and their interactions, as the architectural decisions are made right from the common architecture creation to the individual product architecture derivations. This method is executed in two stages; the first stage focuses on the CA evaluation, while the second stage targets evaluation of individual PAs. This specialization is schematically shown in Fig. 3.3, which illustrates the HoPLAA and its inputs and outputs.

The input to HoPLAA is a bit more comprehensive when compared with the equivalent input required for SPA assessment using ATAM. Architectural drivers are the most crucial behavioural (or functional) and quality attributes requirements of a software system from the perspective of the architecture[Bass et al., 2002]. The architectural drivers determine the shape of an architecture [Clements et al., 2002]. These are extracted from the product line business goals, scope document, and the commonalities and variability of the products, together with the architecture description. It is no surprise that the outputs of HoPLAA are similar to those obtained through an ATAM assessment, since the proposed method is an extension of ATAM. However, the CA evaluation outputs generated in Stage I, such as architecture approaches, evolvability constraints, scenarios, and the like, have to be structured so as to facilitate the subsequent PA evaluation activities in Stage II. Furthermore, HoPLAA places more emphasis on the evolvability points and evolvability constraints generated in Stage I, as opposed to the output obtained through an ATAM analysis of a SPA, as will be explained in the following.

Each of the HoPLAA stages is actually composed of individual steps, seven in stage I and seven in stage II, with each step designed to meet the specific need of the respective target architecture. Stage I is used for evaluation of the common

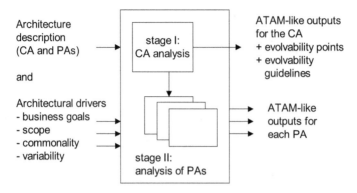

FIGURE 3.3

HoPLAA inputs and outputs. (From F. G. Olumofin, and V. B. Mišić, "A holistic architecture assessment method for software product lines," *Information and Software Technology*, **49**(4):309–323, © 2006 Elsevier B. V.)

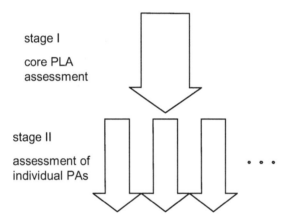

FIGURE 3.4

Pertaining to the stage breakdown of the HoPLAA method. (From F. G. Olumofin, and V. B. Mišić, "A holistic architecture assessment method for software product lines," *Information and Software Technology*, **49**(4):309–323, © 2006 Elsevier B. V.)

architecture and it may equally be used for single product architecture evaluation with little customization. In this respect, CA evaluation in stage I may be viewed as a customized version of the ATAM method. (Note that the ATAM approach, which focuses on the evaluation of single product architectures, consists of nine steps [Clements et al., 2002].) Stage II of the HoPLAA method consists of ATAM-like evaluations applied separately to each individual product architecture, as shown in Fig. 3.4. These evaluations may proceed in sequence or in parallel, depending on the available manpower in the architecture evaluation team.

3.3.2 Extension of quality tradeoff analysis

The notion of architectural tradeoff analysis between two or more quality attributes is among the most prominent features of the ATAM approach [Kazman et al., 1998; Kazman et al., 2000]. Since design decisions at the architectural level have far-reaching consequences, the quality attributes (which are addressed by those decisions) cannot be treated in isolation; almost every decision will affect more than one quality attribute.

Consequently, each design decision involves a tradeoff between two or more quality attributes. The essence of the ATAM approach is to identify those tradeoffs and make them visible to the architects so as to minimize the risks incurred in the architecture definition process. Architectural design decisions that impact quality attribute interactions are classified into sensitivity points and tradeoff points. A sensitivity point applies to a decision about specific aspects of the architecture that may affect—either benefit or impair—at least one quality attribute. A tradeoff point is a sensitivity point between two or more quality attributes which interact in opposing ways [Clements et al., 2002].

Although initially developed for the analysis of single product architectures, the tradeoff analysis is perfectly applicable to product line assessment. When building the CA, design decisions have to fulfill a dual goal. They have to address the quality attributes common to all the variants. At the same time, they have to accommodate quality attributes which may be specific to some of the variants only. Moreover, not all of these variants and, by extension, not all of the associated quality attributes, are known at the time of architecture assessment. So, the architect can only satisfy the common quality goals without making it too difficult to satisfy the product-specific quality goals (some of which are not known) at a later time.

In the HoPLAA method, tradeoff analysis of quality attributes for the CA is performed in stage I, in a fashion similar to the ATAM evaluation but with extra outputs. Further, it extends quality tradeoff analysis to individual PAs in stage II, in order to determine the validity of the quality goals addressed in the CA and also to verify how individual product-specific quality attributes goals are supported. In HoPLAA, tradeoff analysis is not limited to a single architecture, but applies *across* multiple (or two) architectures - that is, between the CA and a PA. To simplify this form of complex qualitative analysis, this research employs a technique based on the relationship between variation points and sensitivity points. It is worth noting that this technique may well find more general applicability in the case of *n*-dimensional and hierarchical product lines [Thompson and Heimdahl, 2001]. The distinguishing characteristic of such product lines is that each PA allows variation points, as does its parent CA, and thus could be instantiated for several other products. By following this technique, the architects could simplify the analysis of tradeoffs in adjacent planes of product line architectures.

3.3.3   Context-dependent scenario treatment

Most single product architecture evaluation methods employ scenarios as the vehicle, both for describing the architecture and eliciting the quality goals for analysis purposes. Once quality attributes and scenarios that exercise them are identified, it is common to eliminate redundant ones and prioritize the remaining ones through voting or other means of reaching consensus amongst system stakeholders. While this procedure may be feasible for SPAs, it becomes cumbersome for large architectures in which the initial number of quality attributes is high, and the number of scenarios may easily be a hundred or more. For product line architectures, the scope is even wider and the numbers are higher.

Hence, the simple scenario generation and voting approach is simply too inefficient and some other way of prioritizing and managing the quality attribute lists must be found. The most obvious one is to use the already existing distinction between the CA and individual PAs as the basis for the complexity reduction. In this manner, it is possible to simplify the management and analysis of the scenarios and focus the evaluation on specific aspects of the product line.

In stage I of HoPLAA, the evaluation team is not constrained on how quality attributes scenarios are generated; not even constraints relating to the commonalities defined by the scope of the product line. In other words, this allows the generation of both common and product-specific scenarios. While the former are analyzed and prioritized in stage I, the latter are recorded but not analyzed until stage II. The reason for this deferment lies in the fact that some of the quality attribute-related scenarios may not be fully known during the generation phase. Instead of trying to get their details no matter what the cost may be, it is more appropriate (and certainly more productive) to allow the architecture evaluation team to freely generate and/or brainstorm all possible scenarios, common and product-specific alike.

Furthermore, the elicitation of some product-dependent scenarios in stage I saves time during the particular product evaluation later on in stage II, and gives indication of possible product-specific quality goals so that architectural decisions made in designing CA will not rule them out. Of course, additional product-specific scenarios are generated, brainstormed, and analyzed during the assessment of a particular PA.

The scrutiny given to quality attributes scenarios generation, classification and prioritization is one of our goals in providing a holistic approach to the analysis of product line architectures. Each stage is focused only on the analysis of those scenarios in the context of the generalized product line architecture or instance architecture under consideration at any one time. More of this will be described in the next section.

3.3.4   Qualitative analytical treatments for variation points

Variation points are architectural placeholders for augmenting the CA with behavioural extensions. They are instantiated as concrete variants in individual product architectures. The reader should recall that sensitivity points are those architectural decisions that affect one or more quality goals [Kazman et al., 1998; Kazman et al., 2000]. For example, the encryption of sensitive message exchange between two components may improve the security quality of a software-intensive system. The architectural decision to introduce cryptographic components between the two communicating components is a sensitivity point to realizing security as far as message exchange between the two components is concerned.

Architectural decisions made in the analysis of the CA in stage I and subsequently found to be the sensitivity points to one or more quality attributes, continue to remain valid for individual product architectures. A possible exception would be the case in which the creation of a PA involves the addition of component variants to those parts of the architecture which interact with the sensitivity points. In the example given above, consider adding a third component to periodically receive exception messages from both components. If such notification messages to this third component are not similarly encrypted, the security of the system may be jeopardized.

An area of the product line architecture which is a sensitivity point and, at the same time, contains at least one variation point, will be referred to as an *evolvability point*. The variation points that could alter quality are specially treated using evolvability points. In particular, we accompany each evolvability point in the CA with a guideline to constrain or guide subsequent PA design decisions and evaluation. The intention is to guard against PA design decisions that could invalidate quality goals already allowed in the CA.

3.3.5   Quality conformance checking technique

A common problem in software product line development and assessment is how to maintain conformance between the CA and the individual PAs, in quality terms. For instance, if a certain quality response of performance is stipulated by the design decisions of the CA, it is highly desirable that none of the PAs deviate from this. This problem is difficult to solve, especially in the evolutionary approach to product line development. In this case, the CA may be derived from exiting products and legacy applications that continue to evolve at the same time as the CA. Despite the different threads of evolution, the existing product architectures and all subsequent PAs should continue to remain in quality congruence with the CA.

The concepts of evolvability points and evolvability guidelines/constraints are explored in [Olumofin and Vojislav B. Mišić , 2005b] to maintain conformance between the CA and the PA. The rationale behind this is the insight that a sensitivity point that interacts with one or more quality attributes poses the greatest challenge in ensuring conformance. The quality attributes of the PA should always remain in conformance with those of the CA when the sensitivity points are located in a mandatory primitive or mandatory composite component. A primitive component [Dincel, Medvidovic and van der Hoek, 2002] is the simplest unit of computation in the architecture. Primitive components can be combined to form composite or complex components. A mandatory component is always present in every PA derived from the CA. It typically encapsulates functions or features common to every product in the product line. However, the above case is not always what is obtained in reality. Oftentimes, there are two or more sensitivity points localized in both areas that have been fully specified (e.g., mandatory components) and areas that are not fully specified (variation point). The architects can only design to fulfill the quality goal of the mandatory component and expect product architects to fulfill their part in designing the variants for the appropriate quality response. If the teams are different, this may be hard to do without duplication of effort.

To ensure conformance of the PA design decisions to those of the CA and, ultimately, to fulfill common quality goals, the pair concepts of evolvability point and evolvability constraint are needed. Note that not every variation point in the CA is an evolvability point – only those variation points that interact with a sensitivity point. The designers of the CA should accompany such evolvability points with appropriate constraints and guidelines. The guidelines help product architects in their work. Evolvability constraint is a statement about an evolvability point that guides product architecture creation in order to fulfill desired quality goals. Just like every other form of constraints, it may be described using the syntax and semantics of an ADL or other constraint language, such as OCL [Warmer and Kleppe, 1999]. Such constraints may restrict variant components in their interaction protocol, internal states, architectural styles, implementation or usage [Medvidovic and Taylor, 1997], in order to fulfill some quality goals.

The combined use of evolvability point and evolvability constraints ensures that the PAs remains in conformance with the CA. Practical examples of the use of evolvability points (EP) and evolvability constraints (EC) are presented in Chapters 4 and 5.

3.4   The Steps of HoPLAA

The common practice for specifying an architecture evaluation method is to outline the steps of activities to perform to arrive at an evaluation result for the architecture. In almost all cases, these steps of activities may be repeated whenever a new architecture is to be evaluated, irrespective of the level of similarity (or dissimilarity) between the architectures being evaluated, e.g., in the case of a product line. Such architectural evaluation methods, although successful for single-product architectures, fail to recognize the duality of the architectures in a product line context. While the product line architecture features commonalities in functional and quality requirements with explicit room for variation points, the product architecture may feature additional functional and quality requirements but generally with no provision for variation points. A one-size-fits-all approach typical of most single product evaluation methods is inadequate in a product line context.

The prescribed steps of the two stages of HoPLAA are presented in this section. Note that the steps may be customized to suit the particular environment of the organization or project team that develops the software product line.

3.4.1 Stage I: CA Evaluation

Stage I consists of the tradeoff-oriented analysis of the core architecture (CA).

I.1 Present the HoPLAA stage I: Present an overview of the HoPLAA and its activities; in particular those of stage I.

I.2 Present the product line architectural drivers: Describe the product line in terms of the motivating business needs, the product line scope definition, and the commonality and variability of the conceived products in the line especially in terms of quality goals.

I.3 Present the core architecture: The architects describe the CA.

I.4 Identify architectural approaches: The evaluation team identifies the architectural approaches used in the architecture. The list is documented but not analyzed. In a product line context, there is need for consistency in the use of architectural approaches throughout the design of the CA and the individual PAs. When the set of architectural approaches used is from a finite known set, the analysis of any architecture in the product line is simplified.

I.5 Generate, classify, brainstorm, and prioritize quality attribute scenarios: Two categories of quality goals can be anticipated on the basis of architectural drivers – those common or mandatory to all products in the line, and those peculiar to some of the products only. The former must be verified in the current stage against the CA, while the latter will be elicited at this stage but will not receive any special treatment until the PA evaluations in stage II. The aim is to have the CA address all quality attribute concern common to every product in the line. Besides, this insures architectural decisions made on the CA do not rule out the achievement of other product-specific quality goals – hence the reason for eliciting product- specific scenarios in this stage.

Note that the quality attribute of variability (also called evolvability or modifiability) should always be analyzed in a CA. The key point here is the need for large-scale reuse of architectures, which is essential to the product line concept itself and is best realized when the variability quality is fully supported by the architecture.

We represent quality attribute scenarios with the utility tree (similar to the ATAM one) in which all possible attribute concerns and associated quality attribute scenarios are shown, irrespective of their generality. In this book, we refer to concrete scenarios addressing the quality-attribute-specific goals of the CA as generic scenarios. Note that these are not the same as general scenarios that 'provide a framework for generating a large number of system- independent but quality-attribute-specific scenarios' [Bass et al., 2002]. In a way, generic scenarios could be considered as system-dependent instances of general scenarios.

We rank each scenario using the indexes of Generality, Significance and Cost, each of which is assigned a value 1, 2, or 3, denoting Low (L), Medium (M), and High (H), respectively. Generality may be mandatory, alternative or optional, with values 3, 2 and 1, respectively; significance denotes how important the quality attribute scenario is to the business driver; and cost is the level of effort or difficulty involved in enhancing the architecture to provide the right responses to the scenario. Once assigned, the values of indexes for each scenario (both generic and product-specific ones) are added up so as to prioritize the list of scenarios.

Using the high-priority scenarios as input, a larger (possibly new) set of scenarios is elicited from the same or different group of stakeholders. Generic scenarios are extracted from the combined list of brainstormed scenarios and prioritized by voting. All other scenarios, both the low-priority generic scenarios and the product-specific ones, are incorporated into the utility tree of the product line for use in stage II. It is anticipated that the most important attribute concerns shared among all products in the line will characterize the scenarios on top of the list.

I.6 Analyze architectural approaches and generic scenarios: Analyze high-priority generic scenarios from step 5 to obtain a set of architectural risks, non-risks, sensitivity points, tradeoff points [Clements et al., 2002], and evolvability points. Evolvability points are those areas in the product line architecture that are either sensitivity points or tradeoff points and that contain at least one variation point. In other words, evolvability points are those areas in the architecture where (a) their composition is associated with at least one variation point, and (b) the associated design decisions affect the realization of one or more quality attribute goals. Associate guidelines to evolvability points to constrain subsequent changes that attempt to move the architecture away from the quality goals already allowed, or to guide future analysis of the PAs that instantiate associated variation points from the CA.

I.7 Present results: A report is prepared for HoPLAA stage I, containing the list of architectural approaches, utility tree, generic scenarios, product-specific scenarios identified, areas of risks in the CA, architectural decisions that are non-risks, sensitivity points, tradeoffs, evolvability points, evolvability guidelines, and risk theme as it affects the product line mission.

3.4.2 Stage II: Individual PA Evaluation

Stage II of the HoPLAA method focuses on evaluation of individual product architectures. Note that the sequence of steps from II.2 to II.7 is repeated for each individual PA.

II.1 Present the HoPLAA stage II: Present an overview of method and give details of stage II. This is a very short step, as the essence of the method should already be known to the evaluation team.

II.2 Present the architectural drivers: Give a brief overview of the CA, the set of driving requirements for the particular PA, and the description of the variable features of this product in terms of functional and quality goals.

II.3 Present the product architecture: Place emphasis only on areas of the architecture that have been recently enhanced through the instantiation of variation points as variants.

II.4 Identify architectural approaches: The architect identifies new or different architectural approaches used in the architecture; these are documented but not analyzed. The architect must give a rationale for every new architectural approach that is used for the design of variants. In addition, the team identifies and documents the specific variation points that have been instantiated as variants.

II.5 Generate, brainstorm and prioritize quality attribute scenarios: Reproduce quality attribute scenarios that are specific to this product from the utility tree generated in stage I, Step 5. Double check to confirm agreement with the quality drivers identified in step 2. In addition, elicit a possibly new set of product-specific scenarios from the same or different group of stakeholders and prioritize the entire list of scenarios by significance (e.g., by voting).

All previously unidentified scenarios may be reflected in the utility tree for the CA; alternatively, a separate utility tree containing scenarios relating to mandatory and product specific quality goals may be created for each PA. The mandatory quality goals may only focus on those quality attributes related to evolvability points whose variation points have been instantiated in this product architecture. The list of variants is used to obtain the affected evolvability points from the results of stage I.

II.6 Analyze architectural approaches: The two classes of scenarios relating to the PA under consideration must be analyzed in this step. The architect must show how generic quality attribute scenarios are not precluded by the product architecture. Generic quality attributes should still continue to be satisfied when design decisions do not violate the evolvability guidelines. If the converse is true, one or more architectural risks have been introduced in realizing the product architecture that may preclude one or more generic quality goals.

In addition, the prioritized product-specific scenarios in step 5 should be analyzed to obtain a set of architectural risks, non-risks, sensitivity points, and tradeoff points. Essentially, the architect must demonstrate how generic scenarios are not precluded in the product architecture design and also how the architecture realizes quality goals that are specific to the product being analyzed.

II.7 Present results: An evaluation report, similar to the one described in stage I, step 7 but without evolvability points and evolvability guidelines (as architecture-based variations are no longer supported), is prepared.

3.5   Evaluation

The concepts and the steps of the HoPLAA method have been described. The next question to be addressed is, how can the HoPLAA solution be applied to PLA assessment problems? And how can one get assurance that the results obtained are accurate and focused on the overall objective of ensuring that the quality goals of the PLA are met?

The answers to these questions can be obtained by conducting actual architectural assessments using the HoPLAA method, and using the results of those assessments as the basis for comparing HoPLAA with existing assessment methods. The results of two such assessments, formulated as case studies, will be presented in subsequent chapters. This use of evaluation-focused case studies to exercise and demonstrate the capability of new methods is a common practice in the architecture assessment methodology community. Each case study involves the assessment of the CA and one PA of a product line architecture. The first of these case studies is a simple case used to demonstrate HoPLAA and illuminates its key features. The second is a more rigorous case study involving a fairly large product line. This was used to determine the capabilities and limitations of the HoPLAA, and to provide useful feedback for evaluating and improving the HoPLAA method.

4

Case Study I: The AGM product line

4.1 Overview

In this chapter, we present the result of the first case study on product line architecture assessment using HoPLAA. The product line in question is the Arcade Game Maker (AGM) Product Line which was jointly developed by Clemson University, Luminary Software and the Product Line Systems Program of the SEI, as a pedagogical product line example. It is made up of three games (Brickle, Pong, and Bowling) to be produced for three different hardware/software platforms (freeware arcade, commercial personal computer, and commercial wireless), for a total of nine products.

Section 4.2 presents a description of the architectural drivers for the AGM product line and some slight changes in quality requirements that have been made to suit this example. To enhance the readability of this book, we only considered the CA and one specific PA for the Brickle game to illustrate the use of HoPLAA. The results of the ATAM evaluation, together with the complete documentation of the AGM CA and other PAs, can be found in [AGMPL, 2004].

4.2 Scope, requirements and qualities

The [functional] commonalities of the game products are: single-player, graphical presentation of games, animation-driven, moveable and stationary game pieces or sprites, and some set of common rules based on physical laws. Mandatory quality requirements for all products are:

1. Performance

   a. The action of the game must be sufficiently fast to seem continuous to the user.

   b. The graphics refresh rate must allow for smooth animations without blurring of graphics.

2. Modifiability

a. A product architecture could be instantiated from the CA in two weeks' time or less.

b. Using the assets of any of the initial products, a single programmer should be able to deliver the next two increments of the products in less than a week.

3. Maintainability

a. The CA and/or PA should not inhibit product updates to newer versions of their environment or platforms as they are released from time to time. Such updates should be completed within three days by a single experienced systems programmer.

The [functional] variability includes rules of the game, type and number of pieces, behaviour of pieces and the physical environment or platform for the games, which could be freeware arcade games, commercial personal computer games and commercial wireless games.

Furthermore, commercial wireless versions of the games are required to support auto-save of game state and scores whenever the user shuts down the game from a pause mode, or powers off the wireless device (such as a cell phone) while the game is running.

For the Brickle product, we associate the usability and performance requirements as an additional (quality) variability. Usability is a crucial requirement in the domain of game programs. One of the business drivers for the AGM product line is to provide users with engaging and interesting games; in fact, a game where users are unable to meet usability problems will not have a second chance. The usability enhancements are as follows:

- Sound support: plays feedback sound which can be set on/off from within the game.

- User-defined customization: replacement of sprites (game pieces) and sound feedback files at run-time.

For the performance quality, the attribute concern is:

- Sound feedback should be provided within 0.75 seconds whenever the puck is in motion, hits the blocks, hit the walls or is hit by the paddle .

This modification introduces variability in quality and functional requirements to the Brickle product architecture.

4.3   Stage I: CA Evaluation

Next, we present the result of the HoPLAA evaluation, starting with stage I – CA evaluation.

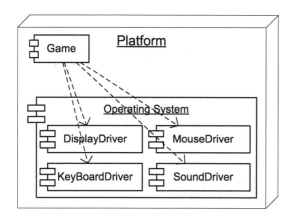

FIGURE 4.1

Enhanced AGM CA deployment diagram .
(adapted from [AGMPL, 2004])

Architecture Description   The CA description has an additional variation point for
a sound device for the Brickle game. The static deployment diagram of the CA is
shown in Fig. 4.1; other views are available in the AGM documentation [AGMPL,
2004].

The *SoundDriver*, shown as a variation point, is the software interface for the
audio device. The Brickles product architecture will feature an audio player variant
for this interface.

Architectural Approaches   Some of the architectural approaches used are the *Model-
View-Controller* (MVC) approach; a modified MVC approach; object oriented specialization and generalization as means to achieve variability; and parameterized
class configuration for variability.

Scenarios   Some of the scenarios elicited are:

i. Performance: Game response time

   1. A paddle hits the puck in response to a user input while the game graphics
   display reflects the effect of the collision in less than 0.75 seconds. (Ranking:
   H, H, H)

   2. Several blocks (stationary sprites) are configured for the Brickles game and
   the start-up time for the game is less than 5 seconds on a PC running a Pentium
   II processor. (Ranking: M, H, M)

   3. The user changes the game speed to the minimum and maximum possible while the systems animations are not jerky and the paddle could still be
   controlled to intercept the puck. (Ranking: H, H, H)

4. A commercial wireless game user in a game session mistakenly hits the power-off button while the game auto-saves its state and scores in 30 seconds before power went down. (Ranking: M, H, M)

ii. Modifiability

1. The AGM Company decides to implement database persistence for commercial wireless game state and scores while a single programmer from the Arcade Team completed an updated CA in three days. (Ranking: H, H, H)

2. The AGM Company decides to field a pinball game that requires more than one view of the game state while the Arcade Team created the PA to use the full MVC in less than one week. (Ranking: H, M, M)

Risks   The following risks were found in the architecture:

i. As the number of stationary sprites grows, the time for collision detection would increase. The architecture approaches collision detection by checking each stationary sprites to determine whether they are being hit by a movable spite.

ii. The cycle time for the animation ticks (managed using the *SpeedControl* Interface) may become too fast for the user to intercept the puck at maximum speed. On the other hand, the ticks that drive animation may have become too slow in a minimum setting to make for smooth motion.

iii. The usability of the game is questionable because the graphics model is rather rudimentary. If the game interface is not satisfactory, it may not have a second chance with users, thereby presenting a negative impression of the company itself.

iv. The current architecture manages persistence by having the game state and scores saved to flat files in its host platform. But the ultimate goal is an architecture that implements database persistence for scores and game state savings. There is the possibility that a single programmer will be unable to deliver the next product increments that use a database for persistence in less than a week. Furthermore, an experienced programmer may require more than three days to migrate from one database platform to another (e.g., migrating from PC-based database client to mobile databases on wireless devices).

Non-Risks

i. The game and score representation is generalized. This could improve maintainability. For example, every game formats its score as a common string.

ii. The game pieces are specialized as movable sprites and stationary spites. The architecture decision to make this separation helps improve the speed of collision detection.

Sensitivity Point(s)

   i. The performance of a game is sensitive to the number of stationary sprites.

   ii. The latency between a user action (e.g., hit the puck) and the update of the game graphics display is sensitive to resource consumption (e.g., CPU, memory) for collision detection and handling. For example, when a brickle puck collides with a pile of blocks, sound feedback is played in addition to the collision handling itself.

Tradeoff Point(s)

   i. Two of the architectural approaches used in the architecture description, namely the MVC and the Modified MVC, introduce architectural tradeoffs. The MVC is extremely demanding in terms of memory, especially for low memory wireless devices, because of duplication of data in the model and views. It is also a performance hog because every change in the model is forwarded to all views. However, it enhances modifiability since separate views may be easily connected to the model. On the other hand, the Modified MVC allows good performance in view updates, but makes it very difficult to create additional views of data (i.e., it opposes modifiability).

   ii. There is a tradeoff between performance and development cost. The architecture currently employs a simple technique for collision detection instead of subdividing the game board into grids to improve the speed of search for collision.

Evolvability Point(s)

   i. The performance of a game is sensitive to the number of sprites in the game board. The number of sprites is a variation point for game products. Hence, the number of sprites is also an evolvability point.

   ii. The sound device is a variation point for implementing sound feedback variants. The fact that this variation point has to do with an area of the architecture that is also a sensitivity point for graphics display response time, makes it an evolvability point

Evolvability Constraints and Guidelines

   i. The number of sprites and their sizes must be controlled based on the environment or platform. A large number of sprites may impair response time for game graphics redisplay. Similarly, pieces that uses large-sized images may deplete memory resources. Smaller numbers of sprites are recommended for commercial wireless games.

   ii. The resource requirements (CPU time, memory and a sound device) for audio feedback should be controlled. Specifically, it must be completed such that total CPU time for graphics redisplay does not exceed the 0.75 seconds limit.

4.4   Stage II: PA Evaluation

A separate architecture description was created for the Brickle product to satisfy functional and quality goals already described. Fig. 4.2 presents the layered representation of this PA.

Scenarios

  i. The Brickle game is running and the sound option is set. The user paddle hits the puck and the system responds with sound feedback in 0.75 seconds.

 ii. The user selects a menu option that turns off the sound, but the sound feedback stops in 1 second.

iii. The game is running and the puck hit the block but the sound plays more than 1 second later.

 iv. The user interrupts the Brickle while running to replace the blocks in the piles with custom-blocks from the *Sprite Library*. The system replaces all blocks in the pile with the custom block and resumes the game correctly.

  v. The user imports a sound clip from the *Audio Clip Library* to replace sound feedback for collision of the puck with the blocks. The game subsequently takes up to 5 seconds to playback the sound clip, placing the sound feedback system out of sync with the game action.

Some scenarios generated in stage I are included in the list of the Brickles PA scenarios.

Scenario Analysis   The Brickles PA realizes two variation points from the CA, i.e., the number of sprites in the game board, and the sound feedback.
    Design decisions needed to implement the variation points affect one or more qualities, and hence are treated as evolvability points. The evolvability constraints in stage I are used to simplify this analysis.

Risks

  i. A user may specify large number of blocks per pile (of blocks) and equally import large-sized images for sprites graphics. This could slow down the animation and action of the game. A low memory wireless device would easily run out of memory for that reason.

 ii. The flexibility of allowing users to provide custom sound clips may result in use of expensive audio clips (e.g., long-playback sound clip) that could place the game action out of sync with sound feedback. The performance goal of the graphics redisplay in 0.75 could be affected as well.

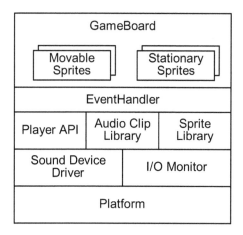

FIGURE 4.2

A view of the Brickles architecture. (From F. G. Olumofin, and V. B. Mišić, "Extending the ATAM architecture evaluation to product line architectures," In *Proceedings of the 5th Working IEEE/IFIP Conference on Software Architecture (WICSA'05)*, pp 45–56, © 2008 IEEE)

Sensitivity Point(s)   Usability of the game as a result of sound feedback is sensitive to the size of audio clips the user is allowed to import.

Tradeoff Point(s)   Enhancing game usability by allowing users to customize sprites, and sounds by importing of the appropriate files could improve games usability but have an adverse effect on performance and memory usage. Some users may use heavy graphics for sprites or may import large sound files.

The risk theme for the PA is to constrain user to specified image sizes and constrain playback time of audio clips. Although this requirement is aimed at improving usability, it could equally inhibit it. The architecture does not currently feature a means for achieving this control. The architecture should also show synchronization techniques for the sound feedback vis-à-vis the game action.

5

Case Study II: The btLine product line

5.1 Overview

This chapter describes the result of the second case study: assessment of a product line architectures called *btLine*. This product line was developed by the systems integration and consulting company B.T. Home Communication, Inc. (the name has been changed for confidentiality reasons). The btLine products were developed to cater to the needs of a group of electronic payment network players, namely financial institutions including banks, merchants, telecommunication organization (i.e., telcos including a GSM network service provider), an inter-bank settlement organization, and a scheme operator. The interoperation of the btLine products form the btNet payment network, which collectively enables remote payment and settlement of financial transactions such as payment for goods and funds transfer.

The delivery channels of transactions to the btNet are WWW, WAP, Mobile Text (or SMS), and XML-based IVRs (voiceXML or VXML). Fig 5.1 illustrates the six currently deployed products of the btLine and their interconnection. The SMS, WAP and VXML channels are delivered to the btMain product via some third-party gateway software applications. For confidentiality reasons, we will only give a cursory description of the CA and the product architecture for btMain, as well as the results of the HoPLAA evaluation.

5.2 Scope, requirements and qualities

The set of common functionality includes the Web-based distributed application model, basic reporting capability, use of cryptography for personal ID security, maintenance of an audit trail, ability to hot list lost or stolen account details, use of parameters and support for configuration management, common user profile management function, payment handling, availability of subscriber, merchant and business-to-business web components, ability to bi-directionally distribute, consolidate and synchronize data, and ability to integrate data from multiple sources.

The set of mandatory quality attributes for all products with which we assessed the CA is as follows.

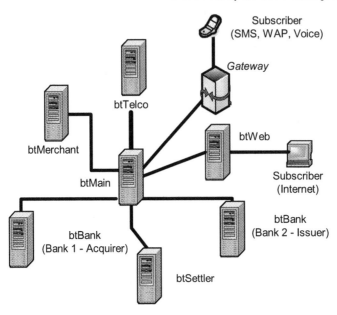

FIGURE 5.1
Topology of the btNet scheme and product interconnections. (From F. G. Olumofin, and V. B. Mišić, "A holistic architecture assessment method for software product lines," *Information and Software Technology*, **49**(4):309–323, © 2006 Elsevier B. V.)

Modifiability/Variability

- Product interactions should be transparent and a product location may be changed without the need to compile or redeploy other components that access it.

- New component addition to any product's architectural configuration must be easy and should not cause ripple effects on the behaviour of existing components.

- New product installation and configuration for a participant joining the btNet should be deployable by a single developer in a single day.

Performance

- Irrespective of the type and number of associated channels, a product must be capable of accepting and processing high-volume and continually arriving requests in a timely manner.

- The payment transaction latency—the time lag between payment initiation from any of the channels and the time when the response is received—should not exceed 60 seconds.

- No btLine product may exceed 20 seconds in its part of transaction processing.

Security

- Any product should be capable of authenticating users and their transactions, and should deny unauthorized access.

- All PINs, passwords, and other confidential information should be encrypted at all times; masked on input, encrypted in memory and in the database.

- An audit trail should be maintained by default for each product.

- Subscriber and merchant account identifications that are reported lost should be lockable from within all products.

Some of the differences between individual products in the btLine include the range of clients that will interact with the product, how payment requests are handled, the number and types of users intended to interact with the product, the interface requirement of the product vis-à-vis the existing systems of the host organization, and other functionalities that are peculiar to each product. For example, the btMain product features the following functional variability:

- Accept request based on WAP, SMS, and VXML protocols besides the default http and https.

- Handle computationally demanding and performance-critical functions like payment, fund transfer, and commission sharing.

- Manage all configurations relating to connecting a new participant to the btNet.

- Serve as a central portal for managing various system functions and data (e.g., subscribers, merchants, banks, telcos, and the settler).

We elicited the following quality variability for btMain from the architecture documentation:

Availability: btMain is the central hub and should not crash. It must be capable of operating continually and be ready to process payments 24 x 7 x 365 with no down time.

Integrability: Its architecture must be open and provide an interface for connectivity with other btLine products, external systems and payment networks.

Performance: btMain must be capable of accepting and processing at least 500,000 transactions per second, originating from any of the payment channels.

Cost-Savings: btMain must be deployable at a minimum cost.

5.3   Stage I: CA Evaluation

This section presents the result of HoPLAA assessment of the CA.

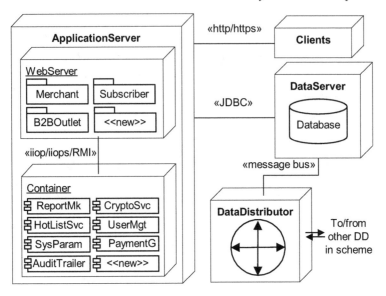

FIGURE 5.2

The CA for the btLine family. (From F. G. Olumofin, and V. B. Mišić, "A holistic architecture assessment method for software product lines," *Information and Software Technology*, **49**(4):309–323, © 2006 Elsevier B. V.)

Architecture Description   The deployment view of the CA is shown in Fig. 5.2. Note the client, application server, data server and data distributor parts of the architecture. The client's default communication protocol with the application server is the http or https protocol. The application server in turn communicates with the data server via the JDBC interface. Similarly, the data distributor middleware communicates the data updates of this data server via a message bus to other data distributors of the btNet scheme.

Accompanying the CA definition is a collection of components, classified as mandatory, alternative and optional, some of which are shown in the deployment view, but will not be discussed further for space constraints. Variation points are denoted with the <<new>> in both the web server and enterprise container. Similarly, the names of the three components *UserMgt*, *SysParam*, and *PaymentG* are typeset in italics to indicate variability, as each of these components features one or more variation points.

Architectural Approaches   Some of the architectural approaches used in the CA are: Three-tier or multi-tier distributed computing architecture; Parameterization as a means of enhancing modifiability; Distributed data repositories and database replication to achieve local access to data; Connection caching and instance pooling to boost performance.

Scenarios Some of the scenarios used for the analysis are:

Modifiability/Variability

- Transparent component access: An improved version of the core payment processor (i.e., PaymentPr) has been installed on a new hardware, with its location parameters configured. And all payment processing agents (i.e., PaymentAg) residing in other products of the btNet could route transaction to the new core immediately without restarting. (Ranking: H, H, H)

- Deploying product for new participant: A new bank indicated their willingness to join the btNet, and a single trained installer, using the btMain product, installed and configured the btBank product for this bank in one day. (Ranking: H, H, M)

- Adding new components or modifying existing ones: Financial regulatory controls now demand that the liability of a bank as a result of transacting on bt-Net platform is limited to the amount of its tendered insurance coverage. The payment processor was updated to carry out this check, and the core payment functions are not affected by the changes. (Ranking: H, H, M)

Performance

- Response time: A user initiates a fund transfer of $100 to his friend via a text instruction, and the transaction completes with feedback received in 10 seconds. (Ranking: H, H, H)

Security

- Authentication: A username and password is requested to access any resource, and the system restricts access to unauthorized users. (Ranking: H, H, M)

- Confidentiality: The database administrator queries the user table (via SQL), and the password/PIN fields are encrypted (or scrambled). (Ranking: H, H, M)

- Activity logging: A user performs some activities on the system after authorization, and the system records the resources accessed. (Ranking: M, H, M)

- Securing lost account details: A user reported a lost btBank card; the card was hot listed and all subsequent transactions involving the card are immediately being declined. (Ranking: H, H, M)

Risks

- For participants that decide to use their application server, data server and data distributor, rather than the default btNet software configuration, more than one day may be required to install and deploy a btLine product.

- The weak point of the parameterization technique used to enhance modifiability is in the data distributor parts; if the data distributor is down, the technique will be ineffective.

Non-Risks

- The user of near real-time asynchronous data replication for synchronizing data servers of different products enhances availability. This guarantees local access to data even in the event of network failure between products.

- The use of caching in three significant places in the architecture improves performance; database connection caching, static web resource caching, and core components instance pooling.

Sensitivity Point

- Design decision on how data is distributed at the database level determines the performance of transactions completed on the btNet.

- The security of transactions is sensitive to the how the data distributors communicate data to the distributed data sources.

- The design decisions on the pooling of heavily used components determine the performance of transactions.

Tradeoff Point

- The localization of a data distributor per data server, while enhancing performance increases the cost of deployment licenses and hardware.

- The maintenance of an audit trail while enhancing intrusion detection and security also introduces performance lag.

- The maintenance of a hot list improves security but hinders performance as a search is made on the list for every financial transaction. The longer the list, the more time it takes to search.

Evolvability Points

- The response time of transactions is sensitive to the number and type of intermediaries between the application server and the channel client (PC browser, mobile phone, wired phone). The fact that the number and type of intermediaries is a variation point also makes it an evolvability point.

- The number of rules driving the operation of a data distributor determines the resources requirements for spawning actionable threads, which determines performance. This is an evolvability point since the number of these rules varies from one product to another.

- The type of user profiles that can be managed from within an btLine product and the data distributor logic that distribute these profiles between products differs. The fact that the security and modifiability quality are allowed by design decision on user profile management also makes it an evolvability point.

Evolvability Constraints or Guidelines

- The number and type of clients that can directly interact with the application server should be considered in light of the timing requirements for transaction response.

- The architects must place consideration on the number of rules to define per data distributor based on hardware resources (CPU and memory). The effective number of rules and the maximum number of interactions with other data distributors must be determined and have PA definitions comply with it.

- The model that presents user profile and system parameters to the user interface must implement appropriate rules to ensure only the right user profile and system parameters can be viewed and changed from within a product. In addition, the routing logic of the data distributors must be carefully designed to avoid transferring the wrong user data or configuration parameters to the data servers.

- To enhance response time for transaction involving a product, external data request from within the product (e.g., balance of a customer account in the host banking system) must not involve complicated and time-consuming queries. Alternatively, an external integration mechanism may be deployed to synchronize account details between the bank systems and their local btLine product; of course with guidance from the B.T. Home Communications team. Better still, outbound request from an btLine product to external systems may be routed to a low-traffic data source or business component for improved response time.

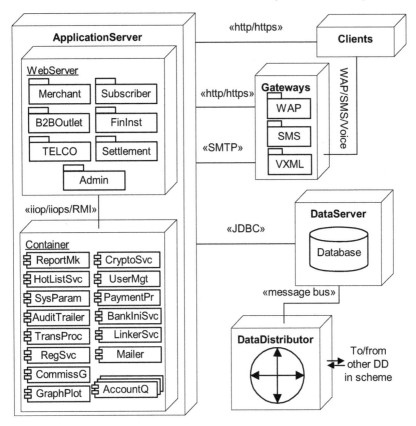

FIGURE 5.3
The product architecture for the *btMain* product. (From F. G. Olumofin, and
V. B. Mišić, "A holistic architecture assessment method for software product lines,"
Information and Software Technology, **49**(4):309–323, © 2006 Elsevier B. V.)

5.4   Stage II: PA Evaluation

For reasons of brevity, we present the assessment of a single PA, the btMain, which
is larger in scope than other architectures in the btLine, including the CA. The deployment view of btMain is shown in Fig. 5.3.

Some of the architectural approaches that can be identified in the PA are: Use of
gateways or filters as an interface between client and application server; two-phase
commit protocol approach for payment processing between two banks; clustering for
high availability and scalability.

The architects' experience on the existing vendor applications and data servers are
reflected in their approach to clustering.

Scenarios   Some of the scenarios used for analysing the btMain PA are:
  Availability

- The primary data server crashes and a switchover to a new primary data server triggers automatically with all client connections transferred, and without loss of any transaction; including those that are open at the time of the crash.

- The hardware running an application server crashes, and user requests are still being serviced.

- The site running a btLine product was destroyed by intentional or natural disaster (e.g., fire) and users no longer receive responses to their requests.

- A btNet telco merchant had to temporarily shut down the SMS service for four hour as a result of scheduled maintenance and btNet users could no longer check their account balance using the SMS channel, for four hours.

Integrability: Interfacing with other systems

- A competitor of B.T. Home Communications has recently deployed a national financial switch for inter-bank transaction facilitation. In order to enjoy mutual advantage from the largely unexplored subscribers' market base, B.T. Home Communications partnered with the promoter of this switch; later, btNet developers successfully interfaced with this switch using the ISO8583 messaging protocol within one month.

Performance: Throughput

- About 500,000 heterogeneous (WWW, WAP, etc.) client requests arrived simultaneously to btMain and each client request is served in less than 30 seconds.

- About 10,000 users initiate transactions from all of the channels (WWW, WAP, VXML, and SMS) simultaneously and the system provides feedback to everyone in less that 10 seconds.

- The btMain is running at peak load, and the settlement organization administrator signed on and initiates a settlement run for the day. btMain could still serve the requests of other users despite the expensive nature of the settlement run; it involves *Settlement* package costly query through the *TransProc* component.

- Bank report personnel log into btMain over the virtual private network to check their total transaction volume for the current quarter, and btMain produced and displays this report within 15 seconds.

Modifiability: Fault correction

- A wrong International Bank Account Number (IBAN) was used to setup a new bank joining the btNet; this affects the data routing logic and the bank particulars defined from btMain. On discovery, this configuration error was corrected within a single day by an experienced installer; in the btMain data server and in the data routing logic the btMain's data distributor.

Risks

- The redundancy techniques of clustering and use of inexpensive RAID disks for data, while enhancing availability can rapidly increase the cost of hardware for supporting such redundancies.

- The current configurations of machines running btMain are on the same local area network; the present lack of an off-site standby facility is a great risk to the $24 \times 7 \times 365$ availability.

- There is currently no redundancy mechanism for the gateways. For instance, an outage of a GSM cellular network service SMSC (Short Message Service Centre) implies outage of the SMS channel of transacting.

- The gateways may limit the system's peak load. The architect did not consider capacities of the various gateways that are to interact with btMain, in determining the peak load. The WWW, WAP and SMS channels are limited by system resources; the VXML channel is constrained by the port density (or number of inbound/outbound telephone connections) of the gateway; which is typically 96 lines (or four T1 connections).

Non-Risks

- The use of gateways bridge various clients to the application server enhances modifiability; since only limited protocol support is required to forward requests to the application server.

- The security and performance quality are enhanced by the use of the two-phase commit approach for payment processing wherein the accounts of the payment parties are checked in real time.

- The architecture addresses the quality of high availability and scalability through clustering.

Sensitivity Point

- The design decisions of the *B2BIntegra* component affects the integrability of btMain with other systems.

- The mechanism for sharing data server connections amongst components is critical for performance.

- Design decisions on the use of clustering for the application server and data replication as a means of redundancy for the data server determines the availability of btMain.

Tradeoff Point

- The data server record-locking granularity affects performance because of the need for resource arbitration amongst components that access data; affects security and integrity of data.

- The used of database stored procedures for some functions invoked by the *TransProc* while enhancing modifiability, could also result in performance loss from contention in database tables accessed during updates.

- The architecture uses a two-phase commit protocol approach wherein a transaction is aborted when the merchant acquirer bank is down. This is detrimental to the goal of rapid return on investment (ROI) or the incentive for profitability on the part of the merchants, even though it enhances accuracy.

Risk Theme: The architects need to consider the impact of the business environment on the architecture more realistically. First, there is need to consider the additional cost of hardware that the clustering technology would introduce and possibly adopt an alternative cost-effective approach for redundancy. Second, the capacity of the various client channels must be analysed to confirm that the load of half a million concurrent requests is feasible. Finally, the architect's approach to replication does not produce a real-time synchronisation result. Other means of real-time synchronization like the use of real-time database messaging should be explored.

6

Comparing architecture assessment methods

The last two chapters have demonstrated the use of the HoPLAA method with an assessment-focused case study. In this chapter, we attempt an objective evaluation of the HoPLAA method. Section 6.1 describes the approach used for this evaluation. The primary objective is the comparison of the HoPLAA and the ATAM. Furthermore, it aims to highlight the differences between HoPLAA and other assessment methods. Section 6.2 presents a comparison of the HoPLAA with the ATAM based on a profile developed in this book, since there is no suitable framework for comparing different PLA assessment methods at the time of this writing. This profile consists of some significant factors or element that may likely be featured in a future framework for the comparison of product line architecture assessment methods. Section 6.3 further compares HoPLAA and ATAM using the parameters from Kazman et al [Kazman et al., 2005]; described in subsection 2.4.4. Section 6.4 and Section 6.5 continues this trend of comparison but using the results and experience of the case studies.

6.1 Approach

One of the most widely used approaches for evaluating the result of computer science research is experimental analysis. For instance, a researcher designs an experiment to compare his or her proposed algorithm to similar existing algorithms for solving a particular problem. This usually involves simulations and some form of statistical analysis and inferences.

Experimental construction is attractive, but, unfortunately, it is extremely difficult or nearly impossible to apply in the context of this research. The HoPLAA solution described in the previous chapter is a method (or methodology) and contains a series of steps. However, the sequence of steps cannot be implemented as a programming algorithm. Irrespective of this, we will attempt an objective evaluation of HoPLAA using a more straightforward analytical technique.

HoPLAA will be subject to three forms of comparison with the ATAM. The first of these will be based on some elements of the NIMSAD (Normative Information Model-Based Systems Analysis and Design) [Jayaratna, 1994]. The NIMSAD is a well known and authoritative reference for creating an evaluation framework for methodologies. Already, two NIMSAD-oriented comparison frameworks have been developed; one for product line development and the other for SPA assessment. The second comparison will use the parameters of [Kazman et al., 2005] that was described in Chapters 2, while the third comparison will be an qualitative description of the performance of the two methods using the results of the case studies presented in Chapters 4 and 5.

For the first comparison, the results obtained from using both HoPLAA and the ATAM will be compared based on some key requirements of product line architecture assessment identified at the inception of this research. Some of those needs are described in Chapter 1 and include: duality of PLAs, variation point analysis, treatment of substantially larger number of scenarios, how the method handles quality interactions with design decisions, and so on.

Although the NIMSAD conceptual (or meta) framework has been used as the basis of comparing methodologies both for scenario-based software architecture assessment [Babar and Gorton, 2004; Babar, Zhu and Jeffery, 2004] and product line development [Matinlassi, 2004], there is currently no comparison framework—based on NIMSAD or other meta framework—for architecture evaluation methods developed for software product lines. The work in [Babar and Gorton, 2004] is an improvement over earlier work [Babar et al., 2004]. It inherits most of the elements from the NIMSAD meta framework which are grouped into method context, stakeholders, structure, and reliability. The ATAM and other single product evaluation methods were compared using the framework developed. However, this framework needs to be extended before it can be applied for the comparison of ATAM and HoPLAA. This extension requires extensive work which offers a promising avenue for future research.

Last comment notwithstanding, a number of factors or elements will be recruited for comparison purposes, drawing from three sources: the two frameworks [Matinlassi, 2004; Babar and Gorton, 2004], and the key research questions that motivated this research. The elements, of which there are no less than ten, are listed in Table 6.1. Note that the profile is not a fully developed comparison framework for product line architecture assessment methods. It is simply a list of elements that we have selected for comparing HoPLAA with ATAM. Of course, the selection was based on the relevance of each element to the problem of PLA assessment.

6.2   Initial comparison of HoPLAA and ATAM

This section compares HoPLAA and ATAM based on the 10-element profile introduced in Table 6.1. The result of the comparison is illustrated in Table 6.2.

Based on the 10-element profile, HoPLAA is specifically designed for PLA assessment, unlike ATAM which is designed for SPA assessment. In addition, HoPLAA not only reveals areas of risk and quality tradeoffs, it also allows for the analysis of

TABLE 6.1

Comparison profile for PLA assessment methods.

Element	Description
Specific goal	What is the primary goal of the method?
Method inputs/outputs	What inputs are supplied to the method and what results are produced by the method?
Variability	Does the method support the analysis of variability?
Quality attributes	Does the method provide guidelines for varying quality lists and prioritization ?
Artifact reuse	What architectural artifacts are created and how are they reused?
Resource requirements	What is the length of time required for the assessment of a product line architecture (core CA and individual PAs)? What is the manpower requirement?
Method structure	What order of steps/stages is used by the method?
Tool Support	Is there tool support for using the method?
Maturity	How mature is the method (inception, development, refinement and dormant)
Comprehensiveness	How thorough is the analysis? How comprehensive or rich is the report/result of an assessment based on the method?

TABLE 6.2

A comparison of HoPLAA vs. ATAM.

Element	ATAM	HoPLAA
Specific goal	Targets SPA assessment by exposing areas of risks and quality tradeoffs.	Assessment of PLAs; reveals areas of risks, performs quality tradeoff analysis and provides guidelines for ensuring quality conformance.
Method inputs/outputs	Inputs: Architectural drivers (key requirements and architecture description). Outputs: Architectural approaches, sensitivity point, tradeoff point, risks, non-risks, risk theme.	Inputs: Architectural drivers (key requirements, scope document, commonality, variability and architecture description). Outputs: ATAM outputs plus evolvability points, evolvability constraints and scenarios.
Variability	Not supported	Analyses variation point qualitatively
Quality attributes	No guideline for handling quality variations and prioritization	Supports variations in quality listing and variations in quality prioritization
Artifacts reuse	Permits reuse, but no specific guidance on product line related reuse	Reuse of several intermediate results- evolvability point, evolvability constraints, scenarios, etc.
Resource requirements	3 days plus time for pre-exercise preparations and summary preparation for each of the CA and the PAs. 4-person team for both PA and CA.	CA assessment takes 3 days and PA assessment takes 2 days. 2 - 4 persons team for the CA and 1 - 2 for the PA
Method structure	Nine steps executed in four phases. The first and the last phases contain no formal step .	Two stages, 7 steps per stage. Each stage is tailored to the requirements of the dual architecture.
Tool Support	Architecture Expert Design Assistant (ArchE) [Bachmann, Bass and Klein, 2003*b*].	Subject of future research
Maturity	refinement	development

quality attribute interactions and conformance across architectures (e.g., the CA and one PA), and not just within a single CA or PA.

The inputs expected by ATAM are a subset of those expected by HoPLAA. This may be explained by the fact that ATAM assumes one-at-a-time development, whereas HoPLAA expects a family development environment. For this reason, ATAM does not tell the assessment team what to do with the extra inputs. Scope, commonality and variability are an essential part of every product line requirement specification. So, there is no extra effort that needs to be expended in putting this together. Also, regarding method output, HoPLAA produces more outputs like the evolvability points and evolvability constraints.

On variability, ATAM provides no guidance whatsoever for dealing with variability in the architecture. This can be either functional (or behavioural) variability or quality variability. HoPLAA provides a means of analysing functional variability represented as variation points. For quality variability, HoPLAA steps and stages are designed to deal with them appropriately.

It is common for different products to possess a varying list of quality attributes. Even for those that have the same list, the order or prioritization of these quality attributes may differ. ATAM does not provide specific guidance here; whereas HoPLAA takes care of individual product architectures possessing differing quality attributes list and prioritization.

Both methods support the reuse of evaluation artifacts like scenarios, utility tree, and analysis models and so on. However, ATAM does not provide specific guidance on product line related reuse.

Stage I of HoPLAA, meant for CA assessment, requires more time to complete compared to an ATAM assessment of the CA. This is because extra outputs, such as the evolvability constraints, have to be produced. However, this is more than compensated for during the individual PA assessment. According to the results of our case studies, HoPLAA will eventually save more time than ATAM for product lines having as little as four individual products.

Furthermore, less manpower is needed for a HoPLAA assessment compared with those needed for the equivalent ATAM one. This is due to the fact that the amount of effort invested in the CA assessment simplifies subsequent assessment of the PAs. On the other hand, applying ATAM to any of the architectures (PA or CA) in a product line requires approximately the same level of effort.

Structurally, ATAM requires more activities (or steps) to be completed that HoPLAA. Each ATAM assessment of a CA or PA will take 9 steps, whereas only 7 steps are needed for HoPLAA assessment of either the CA or PA. Furthermore, HoPLAA steps are designed to be executed consecutively in each of the stages. But the main ATAM assessment steps are broken into two phases with a gap of several days, weeks (or, sometimes, even months) between them [Barbacci et al., 2003]. While this gap arguably enhances the quality of the results obtained, it is obviously detrimental to the overall cost of the assessment. Moreover, additional time is needed to get up to speed in the second phase – time which is effectively wasted since it would not be necessary if the two phases were undertaken in succession.

Of course, the ATAM is more mature compared with HoPLAA, which is still undergoing development. It obviously requires more case study validations to attain the same status of maturity as the ATAM.

6.3   Comparison using parameters from Kazman et al., 2005

Next we present a comparison of HoPLAA and ATAM using the four criteria in Kazaman et al. First, it is important that we mention that HoPLAA is only an extension of the ATAM for software product line architecture. As such, many of the reflections on the ATAM assessment with these four criteria invariably apply to HoPLAA as well. For that reason, this comparison will only focus on clarifying the differences between HoPLAA and ATAM; essentially the aspects that are most relevant to software product line architecture assessment. Readers may safely assume as also holding for HoPLAA any aspects of the criteria, mentioned in the ATAM assessment but that are not discussed in this comparison.

Context and goal   The HoPLAA analysis context assumes a multi-architecture approach or single-architecture-multiple-products approach. This is unlike that of the ATAM that presupposes a SPA or a CA following the single-architecture-multiple-products approach. In a multi-architecture situation, the ATAM has to be applied to the CA and each PA in turns. This is obviously a waste of time since the PAs share some commonalities that are captured in the CA whereas HoPLAA exploits those commonalities to focus individual PA analysis on specific areas or aspect of the architecture.

Further, HoPLAA assumes a product line context in its demand for input the scope, commonality and variability of the product line, in addition to the architecture to be evaluated. These additional inputs required by HoPLAA do not limit its applicability since these inputs are typically by-products of a product line analysis carried our prior to architecture development.

While ATAM can be applied to a SPA at any state (early or late), HoPLAA, in its current status, is best applied on product line architectures under development. The case of applying HoPLAA for a CA where the products already exist still requires further research.

The technique for identifying and recording the goal for the analysis in HoPLAA is similar to that of ATAM. In addition, HoPLAA stage I especially relies on obtaining better clarifications on the goals and possible constraints from an earlier product line analysis process that set the objectives and the scope of the product line development venture. Due to the recognition that the goals or even the order of the goals may differ between products, HoPLAA context is better tailored to product line architecture assessment.

Focus and properties under examination HoPLAA, just like the ATAM, employs quality-attribute scenarios for focusing analysis on specific areas of the architecture. Similarly, the concepts of quality attribute characterizations which provide a codification of the relationship between some quality attributes and the architecture, also applies to HoPLAA.

In addition, HoPLAA uses the concepts of evolvability point and evolvability guideline to focus stage II of HoPLAA on specific areas of the architecture. Also, HoPLAA also takes cognizance of the interactions between quality attribute designed for in a particular architecture (CA or PA) or those designed for in the PA interacting with those of the CA.

Analysis support The emerging concept of tactics which are codified design operations and their effects on quality attributes, and the concepts of quality attribute characterization and utility tree applies to HoPLAA just like it does for ATAM. Certain problem peculiar with the use of tactics is general for both HoPLAA and ATAM. Besides, HoPLAA reuses some branches of the utility tree relating to scenarios discovered in Stage I but that are most relevant to Stage II analysis. Further, evolvability guidelines can be structured in the form of templates to constrain future modifications of the architecture to provide desired quality goals response.

Determining analysis outcomes HoPLAA exposes areas of risks in the CA and in the individual PAs. Just like in an ATAM analysis, the risks uncovered in a particular architecture analysis either directly affect the goals for the evaluation or not. The risks are grouped into themes which points out the quality goals affected by the group of risks. These later goals can be said to tie back to the initial goals of the analysis. However, the determination and interpretation of this form of tie is based on the skill of the analysis team. Also, HoPLAA propagates to every product architecture evaluation the discovered evolvability points and evolvability guidelines; this enhances the speed and repeatability of product architecture analysis.

6.4 Discussion of results for the case study I

Based on the result of the AGM product line case study (See Chapter 4), the main advantages of HoPLAA over ATAM are twofold: first, HoPLAA is streamlined (compared to ATAM) so as to leverage the commonalities encountered in the CA while taking care of variability of individual PAs. This insures more efficient use of the available time – architecture evaluation is expensive and market pressures often impose strict deadlines for architecture development. Further savings can be achieved by reusing some of the scenarios discovered in stage I between individual PA analyses; and trivial but perhaps not quite insignificant savings may be achieved by making step II.1 common to all PAs.

Second, HoPLAA is tailored to fit the requirements imposed by the dual nature of product line architectures. In this manner, it is capable of providing due attention to design decisions that introduce tradeoffs in quality concerns; many of those trade-offs at the level of individual PAs would remain uncovered in the traditional ATAM analysis of the CA. This is accomplished through stage II of the HoPLAA, in which some of the scenarios generated in stage I are reused and the evolvability points and evolvability constraints are used as guidelines to direct the analysis to those areas of the PA that may have changed due to the realization of variation points. For exam-ple, the provision of sound feedback is found to have introduced performance risk to Brickles.

6.5   Discussion of results for the case study II

The result of the btLine product line assessment (See Chapter 5) indicates that the quality attributes and their prioritization significantly differ between the CA and the btMain PA. While the prioritized CA quality attributes are modifiability/variability, performance and security, those of the btMain PA are availability, integrability, per-formance, and cost-savings. Furthermore, the attribute concerns for the quality at-tributes differ between the CA and PA. It is easy to see that conducting the btMain assessment in the context of the CA, i.e., without a separate architecture of its own, would complicate the analysis process and give erroneous results. The separation of a product architecture and its assessment from those of the CA, as espoused by HoPLAA, is therefore well justified.

Another significant benefit of using HoPLAA is its support for variation point analysis. In particular, the architects are 'guided' to those areas of variability in CA that can alter quality attributes responses. For instance, the type of client that inter-acts with the application server is a variation point in the btLine CA; this variation point also determines the response time and, by extension, performance of transac-tions initiated through that channel. For btMain and other PAs that feature variants to provide acceptable response times while not invalidating this common quality, this variation point was analysed, tagged as an evolvability point, and finally associated with constraints or guidelines to guide the PA architecture definition and assessment. (This facility would not be available as part of a regular ATAM assessment.) The use of evolvability points and guidelines insures that product architectures, despite possessing their own separate quality attributes set, do not preclude those qualities set in the CA definition. Evolvability points and guidelines are similarly used in other areas of variations in the CA; the data distributor logic, SysParam usage, and the PaymentG and UserMgt components. On the contrary, the ATAM would only provide guidance for separate analyses of the CA and btMain PA. These, however, would not contain any form of variation point analysis or the relation of qualities in a CA variation point and a PA variant.

Oftentimes, the introduction of a variant to the PA would result in tradeoff between two or more quality attributes, relating to the CA, or the PA or both of them. In the CA, the architects employ parameterization and data replication technique to simplify modifiability. However, in the btMain assessment, this design decision is found to introduce availability and performance concerns; availability concerns are due to the high degree of outages possible with the replication technique, and performance concerns are due to the growth in the number of other products data distributors interacting simultaneously with the btMain. Performance would drop as a result of the high resource demand for running threads in the btMain data distributor. Similarly, the pooling of component instances in the CA is a plus for performance; however, this introduces availability tradeoffs in btMain due to the requirement of half a million peak load. The use of HoPLAA makes more apparent the inherent tradeoffs and sensitivities of quality attributes between a CA and product architectures. None of the current generation of architectural assessment methods, ATAM included, provides this view of vertical interactions among quality attributes in the CA and a PA. We collectively refer to this form of quality sensitivities and tradeoffs between the CA and PA as vertical sensitivity and vertical tradeoff analysis respectively.

We observed that the number of scenarios involved in the analysis of the CA and btMain PA are large, for the following reasons. First, in a product line, there are several architectures (CA and individual PAs), and for each architecture, there are some set of qualities, each of which has a number of attribute concerns. A number of scenarios, relating to specific attribute concerns are required to exercise the architecture. So, the number of scenarios involved in the analysis of product family architectures is substantially larger compared to that involved in the analysis of a SPA. (Note that only a small fraction of the scenarios elicited for the CA and btMain analysis were listed for space constraints.)

However, stage I of the HoPLAA analysis should take less time than the equivalent ATAM analysis of the CA, since some steps have been merged, and the analysis of some scenarios is deferred until stage II. Regarding stage II, steps II.1 through II.3 can be much shorter than their stage I counterparts, since the attendees are already familiar with the procedure. Furthermore, step II.1 can be 'shared' between individual PA analyses, i.e., one session would suffice for product lines with several PAs. In addition, step II.5 will reuse some scenarios already discovered in stage I, giving additional savings. The HoPLAA analysis of a full product line architecture will certainly take more time than the equivalent ATAM analysis of the CA architecture alone, but less time than would be needed to individually apply ATAM analysis to each PA. In either case, HoPLAA out-performs ATAM in terms of comprehensiveness and effectiveness of the analysis, as explained above.

It is perhaps worth noting that stage I of the HoPLAA assessment which is a simplified version of ATAM, could be used for SPA assessment in lieu of ATAM itself. Since it uses seven steps, as opposed to ATAM's nine, and since a SPA does not contain variability points, such analysis could achieve some savings in terms of time and, consequently, cost. In all fairness, those savings will not be spectacular by any measure; still, they might justify the substitution in cases where tight schedule and/or manpower limitations make a regular ATAM assessment too costly.

Also, a scenario will have the most impact on architecture analysis when the scenario is used in the right context of the architecture. For instance, we did not include scenarios exercising the core transaction processing component (i.e., TransProc) of btMain in the CA assessment. It would be out of context since TransProc is an optional component (or feature) in the product line. Similarly, performance-related scenarios on the instance pooling architectural approach of the application server are only used in the CA analysis, since it is a mandatory feature.

7

Conclusions and future work

Evaluating software architectures is an interesting and important activity in the development of quality software products. Evaluation is even more important, from both technical and business perspectives, for a product line development because it relies on reuse of the software architecture. This research has reviewed existing methods for architecture assessment and investigated the characteristics of the product line architectures in particular. The result was used as the basis of extending ATAM, a well known single product architecture assessment method, so that it can be meet the specific requirements of product line architecture assessment. The resulting PLA assessment method, HoPLAA, was described in detail and evaluated through a comparison with ATAM. In this chapter, we will present a summary of this research and outline some promising directions for future work.

7.1 Summary of research

This research reported in this book was motivated by the main thrust of software engineering research: search for methods that will allow the development of software systems with higher quality and productivity. Software is becoming increasingly important and complex. There is a growing need to improve the quality of software systems and also to make the development process more rapid. The emergence of the product line approach holds great promise of realizing these goals. The product line involves a systematic, large-scale reuse of the software architecture. The architecture itself is the appropriate design abstraction for dealing with software quality problems. Whereas the product line concept is noted for improving quality, reducing cost and shortening time-to-market.

However, the design process itself does not warrant the success of a technical product. The product must also be tested or evaluated for its quality and conformance to the original requirements. While the architecture of any sort is not quite a product in the traditional sense, it serves as the foundation for the development of actual products. In the case of product line architectures, the architecture is the foundation for a family of products. This makes evaluation or assessment of such architectures a necessity, more so because design decisions made at the architecture definition phase have far reaching consequences throughout the development cycle. These decisions will ultimately determine the success of the entire family of products. The goal of the assessment process, in the case of architectures, is to ascertain that they can indeed support the quality goals imposed on them and expected from them.

This research reviews a number of approaches to architecture assessment. This includes architecture evaluation methods developed solely for single product architectures (such as ATAM, SAAM, and ARID) and those developed with the product line architecture in mind (example PuLSE-DSSA and VTT framework). We discovered that none of the existing generation of architecture evaluation method has taken the patience to examine the product line concept and the challenges of assessing product line architectures. The review of related work provided insight into a number of questions that must be answered by any architecture assessment method that will fill the place of an architecture-centric, risk mitigating PLA assessment method.

Rather than re-inventing the wheel by developing a new assessment method for software product line from scratch, this research chooses to extend the ATAM method. The ATAM is relatively mature and has a good track record with a substantial number of successful applications in industry.

The main result produced from this research is the development of the HoPLAA method. The HoPLAA method shares its main concepts, most notably the dual form of architecture, larger number of scenarios, and variation points analysis, with the underlying foundations of the product line architecture development approach. The HoPLAA method follows an integrated, holistic approach with two separate, but interdependent analysis steps for assessing both the common architecture of a product line and also the individual product architectures.

The process of evaluating the HoPLAA solution developed in this research is demonstrated through two case studies. The first case study, the smaller of the two, demonstrated how to evaluate an architecture with HoPLAA. The second case study involves a large industrial product line. Then, the results of the HoPLAA evaluation were compared to those obtained with ATAM. While a suitable framework for comparing product line architecture assessment methods is yet to appear, this research creates a list of elements or factors and used it for this purpose. Developing a comprehensive framework for comparison and assessment of product line architecture assessment methods is another promising avenue for future work.

The results obtained in this manner show it is more advantageous to use HoPLAA instead of ATAM for PLA assessment. At a more general level, the HoPLAA method compares favorably with other assessment methods which are capable of CA assessment. HoPLAA offers a more general approach than PuLSE-DSSA [DeBaud et al., 1998; Bayer et al., 2000], as it can be used regardless of the particular development methodology. Its results are also more useful, as they provide more product line-specific information. HoPLAA could also prove feasible within the PLA evaluation framework developed by the VTT Technical Research Centre of Finland [Dobrica and Niemelä, 2000].

In terms of efficiency, it was found that the HoPLAA analysis of a product line architecture would take more time than the equivalent ATAM analysis of the core architecture alone, but less time than would be needed to perform the ATAM analysis to each individual product architecture separately. In either case, HoPLAA out-performs ATAM in terms of comprehensiveness and effectiveness of the analysis, as explained above.

7.2 Future work

The result obtained from the use of the HoPLAA presented is impressive, but definitely not sufficient. HoPLAA requires further validation and refinements through more focused case studies. As HoPLAA is applied to real-life case studies, its areas of weaknesses will be discovered and research effort will be appropriately directed to remedy the defects. ATAM is today classified as a relatively mature method [Babar and Gorton, 2004]. HoPLAA will need to be exercised with several additional industrial case studies to be classified at that level.

Another future work is the development of a comparison framework for PLA assessment methods. Such a framework will simplify the comparison of HoPLAA with future assessment methods that will be developed in this direction. Besides, it will help industrial users of assessment methodology decide on the capabilities of assessment methods being offered.

Also, there is currently a severe shortage of product line architecture examples to be used as benchmarks for methodology development. As at the time of this writing, there is just one academic example (i.e., the AGM product line) of a complete product line documentation. This work can contribute further by developing an example product line architecture for use in this research area. The higher the number of available examples, the easier it will be to develop and compare methodologies, and train prospective users.

Finally, HoPLAA, ATAM and several other existing scenario-based methods generally classified as qualitative assessment techniques are but first steps in the route toward developing a comprehensive assessment framework for software architectures. There is also a need to accompany them with quantitative or measurement-based techniques closely related to metrics for PLA assessment. This is a wideopen research area that can be pursued as future work.

7.3 Conclusions

The systematic, large-scale reuse of the architecture is at the core of the product line approach to software development. But before successful reuse is possible, the PLA must be correctly developed and assessed. While the problems of product line architecture development have been addressed with some impressive results, the assessment of the product line architectures has been based on methods developed for single product architectures. The complexity of evaluating product line architecture like the dual form of the architectures, existence of variation points, the need for associating context with the large number of quality attributes scenarios and the need to perform quality tradeoff analysis across the PLAs have largely been ignored.

This research investigates the characteristics of the dual architectures in a product line context with the view of developing a product line assessment method. The result of the investigations were directed to extend the popular ATAM with suitable concepts and techniques to form the HoPLAA method. HoPLAA proposes a holistic approach for comprehensively analyzing the product line architecture and the individual product architectures. The use of HoPLAA for the assessment of PLAs offers distinct advantages as described in the results of two case studies that were conducted in the course of this research. The proposed HoPLAA can be regarded as a candidate method to fill the present vacuum created by the lack of an inexpensive, architecture-centric, and risk mitigating PLA assessment method. HoPLAA allows for systematic reuse of scenarios and other analysis results; it provides more comprehensive analysis; focuses better on architecture evaluation of product lines and results in more efficient evaluation.

Having a comprehensive assessment method for PLA is a major step forward in making architecture-centric development of software product lines practical and beneficial. Lastly, the long chase of software engineering towards improved software quality and development productivity will gradually pay off as HoPLAA and subsequent PLA assessment methods that will be developed mature. It is our expectation that the work done in this research will help advance software engineering towards this promise.

List of Abbreviations

ADL   Architecture Description Language

ADR   Active Design Reviews

AGM   Arcade Game Maker

ANSI   American National Standards Institute

ARID   Active Reviews for Intermediate Design

ATAM   Architecture Tradeoff Analysis Method

CA   Core Architecture

CBAM   Cost Benefit Analysis Method

FEF   Family Evaluation Framework

HoPLAA   Holistic Product Line Architecture Assessment

IBAN   International Bank Account Number

IEC   International Electrotechnical Commission

IEEE   Institute of Electrical and Electronics Engineers

IESE   Fraunhofer Institute for Experimental Software Engineering

ISO   International Organization for Standardization

ITEA   Information Technology for European Advancement

IVR   Interactive Voice Response

JDBC   Java Database Connectivity

MDA   Model Driven Architecture

NIMSAD   Normative Information Model-Based Systems Analysis and Design

PA   Product Architecture

PIN   Personal Identification Number

PLA   Product Line Architecture

PuLSE − DSSA Product Line Software Engineering - Domain-Specific Software
        Architecture

RUP   Rational Unified Process

SAAM Software Architecture Analysis Method

SEI   Software Engineering Institute

SMS   Shot Message Service

SPA   Single Products Architecture

SPE   Software Performance Engineering

TRC   Technical Research Centre of Finland

UML   Unified Modelling Language

VTT   Valtion Teknillinen Tutkimuskeskus Technical Research Centre of Finland

VXML voiceXML

WAP   Wireless Application Protocol

WWW World Wide Web

XML   eXtensible Markup Language

References

AGMPL [2004], *Arcade Game Maker Product Line*, The Product Line Systems Program of the Software Engineering Institute, Luminary Software and Clemson University Dept of Computer Science. available at http://www.cs.clemson.edu/~johnmc/.

Babar, M. A. and Gorton, I. [2004], Comparison of scenario-based software architecture evaluation methods., *in* 'APSEC', pp. 600–607.

Babar, M. A., Zhu, L. and Jeffery, D. R. [2004], A framework for classifying and comparing software architecture evaluation methods., *in* 'Australian Software Engineering Conference', pp. 309–319.

Bachmann, F., Bass, L. and Klein, M. [2003*a*], Moving from quality attribute requirements to architectural decisions, *in* 'Proceedings of STRAW '03', pp. 346–352.

Bachmann, F., Bass, L. and Klein, M. [2003*b*], Preliminary design of arche: A software architecture design assistant, CMU SEI Technical Report CMU/SEI-2003-TR-021, Software Engineering Institute, Pittsburgh, PA.

Barbacci, M., Clements, P., Lattanze, A., Northrop, L. and Wood, W. [2003], Using the Architecture Tradeoff Analysis Method (ATAM) to evaluate the software architecture for a product line of avionics systems: A case study, CMU SEI Technical Note CMU/SEI-2003-TN-012, Software Engineering Institute, Pittsburgh, PA.

Bass, L., Clements, P. and Kazman, R. [2002], *Software Architecture in Practice*, The SEI Series in Software Engineering, 2nd edn, Addison-Wesley, Reading, MA.

Bayer, J., Anastasopoulos, Gacek, C. and Flege, O. [2000], A process for product line architecture creation and evaluation: PuLSE-DSSA version 2.0, Technical Report No.038.00/E, Fraunhofer IESE, Kaiserslautern, Germany.

Boehm, B. W. [1981], *Software Engineering Economics*, Prentice Hall, Upper Saddle River, NJ.

Boehm, B. W., Brown, J. R. and Lipow, M. [1976], Quantitative evaluation of software quality, *in* 'ICSE'76: Proc. of the 2nd Int. Conf. on Software engineering', San Francisco, CA, pp. 592–605.

Bosch, J. [2000], *Design & Use of Software Architectures*, Addison-Wesley, Harlow, England.

Bosch, J. [2002], Maturity and evolution in software product lines: Approaches, artefacts and organization, *in* 'SPLC 2: Proceedings of the Second International Conference on Software Product Lines', Springer-Verlag, London, UK, pp. 257–271.

Chrissis, M. B., Konrad, M. and Shrum, S. [2003], *CMMI: Guidelines for Process Integration and Product Improvement*, The SEI Series in Software Engineering, Addison-Wesley, Reading, MA.

Clements, P., Kazman, R. and Klein, M. [2002], *Evaluating Software Architectures – Methods and Case Studies*, The SEI Series in Software Engineering, Addison-Wesley, Reading, MA.

Clements, P. and Northrop, L. [2002], *Software Product Lines*, The SEI Series in Software Engineering, Addison-Wesley, Reading, MA.

Clements, P. and Northrop, L. [2005], *A Framework for Software Product Line Practice Version 4.2*, Software Engineering Institute.
URL: *http://www.sei.cmu.edu/productlines/framework.html*

Dashofy, E. M., der Hoek, A. V. and Taylor, R. N. [2001], A highly-extensible, xml-based architecture description language, *in* 'WICSA '01: Proceedings of the Working IEEE/IFIP Conference on Software Architecture (WICSA'01)', IEEE Computer Society, Washington, DC, USA, p. 103.

DeBaud, J.-M., Flege, O. and Knauber, P. [1998], PuLSE-DSSA: a method for the development of software reference architectures, *in* 'ISAW '98: Proc. Third Int. Workshop on Software Architecture', Orlando, FL, pp. 25–28.

Dijkstra, E. W. [1968], 'The structure of the 'THE'-multiprogramming system', *Commun. ACM* **11**(5), 341–346.

Dincel, E., Medvidovic, N. and van der Hoek, A. [2002], Measuring product line architectures, *in* 'PFE '01: Revised Papers from the 4th International Workshop on Software Product-Family Engineering', Springer-Verlag, London, UK, pp. 346–352.

Dobrica, L. and Niemelä, E. [2000], A strategy for analyzing product line software architectures, Technical Report VTT-PUBS-427, VTT Electronics, Oulu, Finland.

Dobrica, L. and Niemelä, E. [2002], 'A survey on software architecture analysis methods', *IEEE Transactions on Software Engineering* **28**(7), 638–653.

Garlan, D. [2000], Software architecture: a roadmap, *in* 'ICSE'00: Proc. 22nd Int. Conf. Software Engineering', Limerick, Ireland, pp. 91–101.

Garlan, D. [2001], Software architecture, *in* J. Marciniak, ed., 'Wiley Encyclopedia of Software Engineering', John Wiley & Sons, New York, NY.

Garlan, D., Monroe, R. and Wile, D. [1997], Acme: an architecture description interchange language, *in* 'Proc. 1997 Conf. of the Centre for Advanced Studies on Collaborative research', Toronto, ON, pp. 7–21.

Giannakopoulou, D. and Magee, J. [2003], Fluent model checking for event-based systems, *in* 'ESEC/FSE-11: Proceedings of the 9th European software engineering conference held jointly with 11th ACM SIGSOFT international symposium on Foundations of software engineering', ACM Press, New York, NY, USA, pp. 257–266.

Hassan, A. E. and Holt, R. C. [2000], A reference architecture for web servers, *in* 'WCRE '00: Proceedings of the Seventh Working Conference on Reverse Engineering (WCRE'00)', IEEE Computer Society, Washington, DC, USA, p. 150.

Hofmeister, C., Nord, R. and Soni, D. [1999], *Applied Software Architecture*, Addison-Wesley.

IEEE [2000], *Recommended Practice for Architectural Description of Software-Intensive Systems*, IEEE Std 1471-2000 edn, Institute of Electrical and Electronics Engineers, New York, NY.

ISO/IEC [2001], *Software Engineering - Product Quality - Part 1: Quality Model*, iso/iec standard 9126-1 edn, ISO/IEC.

Jayaratna, N. [1994], *Understanding and Evaluating Methodologies: NIMSAD, a Systematic Framework*, McGraw-Hill, Inc., New York, NY, USA.

Jazayeri, M., Ran, A. and van der Linden, F. [2000], *Software architecture for product families: principles and practice*, Addison-Wesley Longman, Boston, MA.

Kazman, R., Abowd, G., Bass, L. and Clements, P. [1996], 'Scenario-based analysis of software architecture', *IEEE Software* 13(6), 47–55.

Kazman, R., Asundi, J. and Klein, M. [2002], Making architecture design decisions: An economic approach, CMU SEI Technical Note CMU/SEI-2002-TR-035, ADA408740, Software Engineering Institute, Pittsburgh, PA.

Kazman, R., Bass, L., Klein, M., Lattanze, T. and Northrop, L. [2005], 'A basis for analyzing software architecture analysis methods', *Software Quality Control* 13(4), 329–355.

Kazman, R., Bass, L., Webb, M. and Abowd, G. [1994], SAAM: a method for analyzing the properties of software architectures, *in* 'ICSE '94: Proc. 16th Int. Conf. Software Engineering', Sorrento, Italy, pp. 81–90.

Kazman, R. and Carrière, S. J. [1999], 'Playing detective: Reconstructing software architecture from available evidence', *Automated Software Engineering* 6(2), 107–138.

Kazman, R., Klein, M., Barbacci, M., Longstaff, T., Lipson, H. and Carriere, J. [1998], The architecture tradeoff analysis method, *in* 'Proc. ICECCS '98', Monterey, CA, pp. 68–78.

Kazman, R., Klein, M. and Clements, P. [2000], ATAM: Method for architecture evaluation, CMU SEI Technical Note CMU/SEI-2000-TR-004, ADA382629, Software Engineering Institute, Pittsburgh, PA.

Kazman, R., Kruchten, P., Nord, R. L. and Tomayko, J. E. [2004], Integrating software-architecture-centric methods into the Rational Unified Process, CMU SEI Technical Note CMU/SEI-2004-TR-011, Software Engineering Institute, Pittsburgh, PA.

Khare, R., Guntersdorfer, M., Oreizy, P., Medvidovic, N. and Taylor, R. [2001], xadl: Enabling architecture-centric tool integration with xml, *in* 'HICSS '01: Proceedings of the 34th Annual Hawaii International Conference on System Sciences (HICSS-34)-Volume 9', IEEE Computer Society, Washington, DC, USA, p. 9053.

Kim, S. D., Chang, S. H. and La, H. J. [2005], A systematic process to design product line architecture., *in* 'ICCSA (1)', pp. 46–56.

Kruchten, P. B. [1995], 'The 4+1 view model of architecture', *IEEE Software* **12**(6), 42–50.

Magee, J., Dulay, N., Eisenbach, S. and Kramer, J. [1995], Specifying distributed software architectures, *in* 'Proceedings of the 5th European Software Engineering Conference', Springer-Verlag, London, UK, pp. 137–153.

Malveau, R. C. [2000], *Software Architect Bootcamp: A Programmer's Field Manual*, Prentice Hall, Upper Saddle River, NJ.

Matinlassi, M. [2004], Comparison of software product line architecture design methods: Copa, fast, form, kobra and qada, *in* 'ICSE '04: Proceedings of the 26th International Conference on Software Engineering', IEEE Computer Society, Washington, DC, USA, pp. 127–136.

Medvidovic, N., Rosenblum, D. S., Redmiles, D. F. and Robbins, J. E. [2002], 'Modeling software architectures in the unified modeling language', *ACM Trans. Softw. Eng. Methodol.* **11**(1), 2–57.

Medvidovic, N. and Taylor, R. N. [1997], A framework for classifying and comparing architecture description languages, *in* 'ESEC'97/FSE-5: Proc. 6th European Conf. held jointly with the 5th ACM SIGSOFT Int. Symp. Foundations of Software Engineering', Zurich, Switzerland, pp. 60–76.

Medvidovic, N. and Taylor, R. N. [2000], 'A classification and comparison framework for software architecture description languages', *IEEE Transactions on Software Engineering* **26**(1), 70–93.

Mitchell, B. S., Mancoridis, S. and Traverso, M. [2002], Search based reverse engineering, *in* 'SEKE '02: Proceedings of the 14th international conference on Software engineering and knowledge engineering', ACM Press, New York, NY, USA, pp. 431–438.

Niemelä, E., Matinlassi, M. and Taulavuori, A. [2004], Practical evaluation of software product family architectures, *in* 'Proc. Third Software Product Line Conference SPLC 2004', Boston, MA, pp. 130–145.

Nord, R. L., Barbacci, M. R., Clements, P., Kazman, R., Klein, M., O'Brien, L. and Tomayko, J. E. [2003], Integrating the Architecture Tradeoff Analysis Method (ATAM) with the cost benefit analysis method (CBAM), CMU SEI Technical Note CMU/SEI-2003-TN-038, Software Engineering Institute, Pittsburgh, PA.

Olumofin, F. G. and Mišić, V. B. [2007], 'A Holistic Architecture Assessment Method for Software Product Lines', *Information and Software Technology* **49**(4), 309–323.

Olumofin, F. G. and Vojislav B. Mišić [2005a], Extending the ATAM Architecture Evaluation to Product Line Architectures, *in* 'WICSA 5: Proceedings of the 5th Working IEEE/IFIP Conference on Software Architecture', Pittsburgh, PA.

Olumofin, F. G. and Vojislav B. Mišić [2005b], Quality-Driven Conformance Checking in Product Line Architectures, *in* 'R2PL 2005: Proceedings of the First International Workshop on Reengineering towards Product Lines', Pittsburgh, PA.

OMG [2003], *MDA-Guide*, v1.0.1 edn, Object Management Group, omg/03-06-01.

Parnas, D. L. [1972], 'On the criteria to be used in decomposing systems into modules', *Commun. ACM* **15**(12), 1053–1058.

Parnas, D. L. [1978], Designing software for ease of extension and contraction, *in* 'ICSE '78: Proc. 3rd Int. Conf. Software engineering', pp. 264–277.

Parnas, D. L. and Weiss, D. M. [1985], Active design reviews: principles and practices, *in* 'ICSE '85: Proceedings of the 8th international conference on Software engineering', IEEE Computer Society Press, Los Alamitos, CA, USA, pp. 132–136.

RUP [2001], *Rational Unified Process*.

Shaw, M. and Garlan, D. [1996], *Software Architecture: Perspectives on an Emerging Discipline*, Prentice Hall, Englewood Cliffs, NJ.

Simon, D. and Eisenbarth, T. [2002], Evolutionary introduction of software product lines, *in* 'SPLC 2: Proceedings of the Second International Conference on Software Product Lines', Springer-Verlag, London, UK, pp. 272–282.

Smith, C. U. [1990], *Performance Engineering of Software Systems*, Addison-Wesley Longman Publishing Co., Inc., Boston, MA, USA.

Staff, C. [1998], *IEEE Standard for a Software Quality Metrics Methodology*, ieee 1061-1998 edn.

Staples, M. and Hill, D. [2004], Experiences adopting software product line development without a product line architecture, *in* 'APSEC '04: Proceedings of the 11th Asia-Pacific Software Engineering Conference (APSEC'04)', IEEE Computer Society, Washington, DC, USA, pp. 176–183.

Svahnberg, M. and Bosch, J. [2000], Issues concerning variability in software product lines, *in* 'IW-SAPF-3: Proceedings of the International Workshop on Software Architectures for Product Families', Springer-Verlag, London, UK, pp. 146–157.

Svahnberg, M., Wohlin, C., Lundberg, L. and Mattsson, M. [2002], A method for understanding quality attributes in software architecture structures, *in* 'SEKE '02: Proceedings of the 14th international conference on Software engineering and knowledge engineering', ACM Press, New York, NY, USA, pp. 819–826.

Thompson, J. M. and Heimdahl, M. P. E. [2001], Extending the product family approach to support n-dimensional and hierarchical product lines, *in* 'Proc. Fifth IEEE Int. Symp. Requirements Engineering (RE'01)', Washington, DC, p. 56.

van der Linden, F., Bosch, J., Kamsties, E., Känsälä, K., Krzanik, L. and Obbink, J. H. [2003], Software product family evaluation, *in* 'PFE', pp. 352–369.

van der Linden, F., Bosch, J., Kamsties, E., Känsälä, K. and Obbink, J. H. [2004], Software product family evaluation, *in* 'Proc. Third Software Product Line Conference SPLC 2004', Boston, MA, pp. 110–129.

Warmer, J. and Kleppe, A. [1999], *The object constraint language: precise modeling with UML*, Addison-Wesley Longman Publishing Co., Inc., Boston, MA, USA.

Weiss, D. M. and Lai, C. T. R. [1999], *Software Product-Line Engineering – A Family-Based Software Development Process*, Addison-Wesley, Reading, MA.

Woods, E. and Rozanski, N. [2005], Using Architectural Perspectives, *in* 'WICSA 5: Proceedings of the 5th Working IEEE/IFIP Conference on Software Architecture', Pittsburgh, PA.

Index

Active Reviews for Intermediate Design
  (ARID), 17
algorithm, 1
Application engineering, 13
Architectural approaches, 35, 39
Architectural decisions, 31
Architectural styles, *see* Styles
architecture, *see* Software architecture
Architecture analysis, *see* Architecture
  assessment
Architecture assessment, 2
  Approaching PLA assessment, 26
  Problems of product line, 5
  SPA assessment, 14
Architecture business cycle, 10
Architecture Description Language, 11
Architecture evaluation, *see* Architecture
  assessment
Architecture reconstruction, 12
Architecture Tradeoff Analysis Method
  (ATAM), 16, 22
  inputs, outputs, participants, 22
  output, 25
  steps, 22
attribute concerns, 9

btLine, 45

Capability Maturity Model Integration,
  19
Checking technique, 31
Common architecture, 2
Commonalities, 5, 37
Comparison profile, 58
component, 1
conformance checking, 8
connector, 1

COPA, 13
core architecture, 5
Core asset, 2, 12
Cost Benefit Analysis Method (CBAM),
  17

data structure, 1
Design artifacts, 2
Domain engineering, 13
dual form, 5, 6

Evolvability constraint, *see* Evolvability
  guideline
Evolvability guideline, 31, 35
Evolvability point, 31, 34, 35, 41

Family Evaluation Framework (FEF), 19
FAST, 13
FORM, 13

Generic quality attributes, 35

Holistic approach, 27
Holistic Product Line Architecture Assessment, 3, 20
  concepts, 27
  dual stages, 28
  evaluation, 35
  inputs and outputs, 27
  stage I, 33
  stage II, 34
  steps, 32

Idioms, *see* Styles
information hiding, 10

KobrA, 13

meta, 58

modularity, 10

NIMSAD, 19
Non-Risks, 40

Perspectives, 11
PLA evaluation framework, 19
product architectures, 5
Product families, *see* Software product
    lines
Productivity, 12
productivity, 1
PuLSE-DSSA, 18

QADA, 13
Quality, *see* software quality
Quality attribute interactions, 6
    horizontal, 7
    vertical, 7
quality attributes, *see* Software quality
Quality attributes scenarios, 6

Re-engineering, 12
Reuse, 1, 12
    Architecture-based, 1
Reverse engineering, 12
Risk theme, 55
Risks, 40, 42

Scenario
    Context-dependent treatment, 30
    Prioritization, 23
Scenarios, 6, 14, 39, 42
    alternative, 6
    Direct scenarios, 15
    environment, 14
    Indirect scenarios, 15
    mandatory, 6
    optional, 6
    response, 14
    stimulus, 14
sensitivities, *see* sensitivity point
sensitivity point, 7, 29, 41, 43
    vertical, 29
Software architecture, 1, 9
    abstractions, 1

Assessing methods, 19
attributes, 9
definition, 3
development, 10
roles, 4
Single product architectures, 2
Software Architecture Analysis Method
    (SAAM), 14
Software product lines, 2, 12
    definition, 4
    evolutionary approach, 4
    PLA assessment, 17
    revolutionary approach, 4
Software quality, 9
    evolution, 9
    execution, 9
Styles, 10

Tactics, 10
topology, 1
tradeoff point, 7, 29, 41, 43
    vertical, 29
tradeoffs, *see* tradeoff point

Unified Modelling Language, 11
Utility tree, 22, 35

variability, 5
variants, 5
variation point, 5, 6, 8
    analytical treatment, 30
View, 10
    4+1 model, 10
    significance, 10
Viewpoints, 11

www.ingramcontent.com/pod-product-compliance
Lightning Source LLC
LaVergne TN
LVHW080102070326
832902LV00014B/2372